VICTORIAN LACE CROCHET
38 EXQUISITE DESIGNS FOR THE HOME

THE VANESSA-ANN COLLECTION

Ballantine Books • New York

Produced for **Ballantine Books** by **The Vanessa-Ann Collection**

Owners: TERRECE BEESLEY WOODRUFF
and JO PACKHAM

Staff: CARRIE ALLEN
GLORIA BAUR
VICKI BURKE
CHRISTINE DEETER
KRISTEN JARCHOW
SUSAN JORGENSEN
MARLENE LUND
MARGARET MARTI
BARBARA MILBURN
PAMELA RANDALL
JULIE TRUMAN
NANCY WHITLEY

The photography for this book was done at:

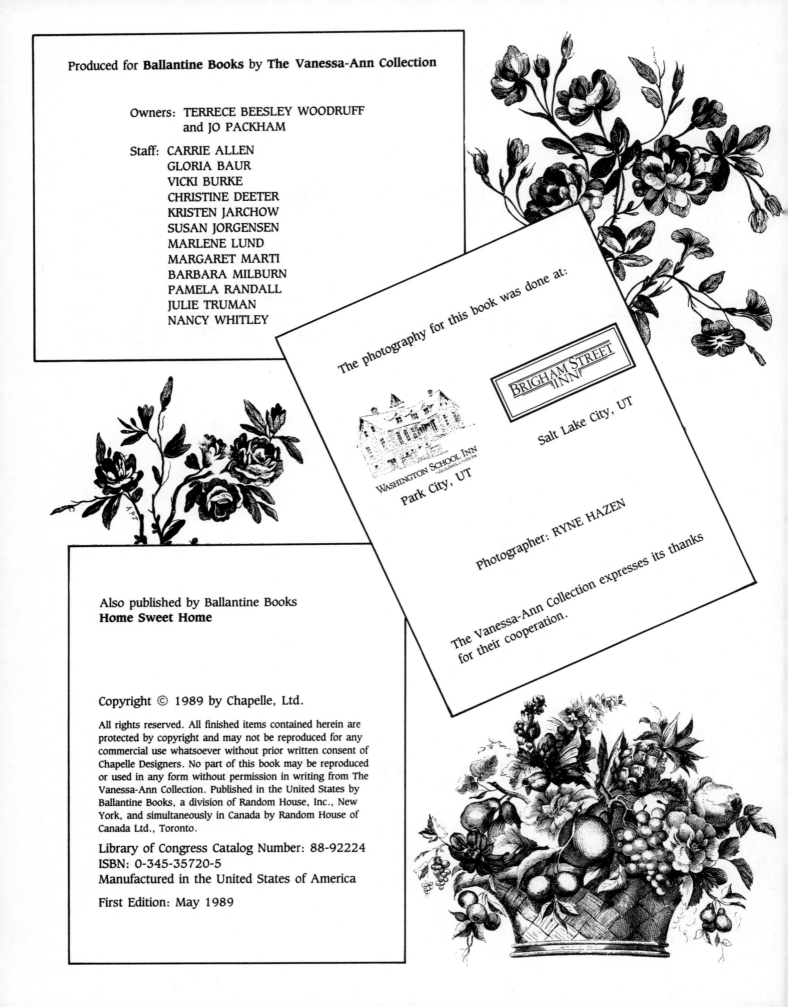

WASHINGTON SCHOOL INN
An Authentic Country Inn
Park City, UT

BRIGHAM STREET INN
Salt Lake City, UT

Photographer: RYNE HAZEN

The Vanessa-Ann Collection expresses its thanks
for their cooperation.

Also published by Ballantine Books
Home Sweet Home

Library of Congress Catalog Number: 88-92224
ISBN: 0-345-35720-5
Manufactured in the United States of America

First Edition: May 1989

Michael,

Thank you for asking me to dance and then teaching me how.

I love you.

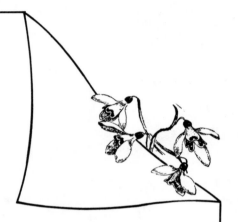

Life in the Victorian days had its own quality and charm. It was a simpler and a more quiet time, a time many of us yearn for today.

For this reason, we have designed this beautiful collection of crochet designs to recreate the essence of that bygone era with today's know-how. From a dainty linen doily to simply exquisite Christmas ornaments, here is an abundant array of projects for you to choose from.

You might share them with friends or family, or consider using them to create a romantic display in your own home. Whatever you decide, now is the time to delight in crocheting these special treasures.

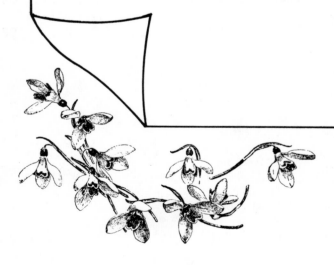

Contents

Baby's Douvet

MATERIALS:

Coats & Clark's Variegated Pink - 5 balls (250 yards per ball)

Coats & Clark's –30 White - 1 ball (350 yards per ball)

Coats & Clark's –30 Green - 1 ball (250 yards per ball)

Size 7 steel hook

Size 10 steel hook

Edging: 16 flower squares (use size 7 hook) For afghan, make 336 ch links (116″), for pillow, make 64 ch links (24″). To make ch link: ch 3, dc in first ch made, * ch 3, dc between ch 3 and dc, (2 links made) repeat from * until desired number of ch links are made. Turn, work on dc side of link.

Row 1: (Beading row) Sl st in first link, ch 4, dc in same link, * ch 1, (dc, ch 1, dc) in next link. (Shell made). Repeat from * across.

Row 2: (Beading row) Ch 1, turn, * 2 sc in next ch-1 sp. Repeat from * across, turn.

Row 3: Ch 3, 3 dc in first sc, sk 5 scs, sc in next sc, * ch 3, 3 dc in same st as sc, sk 4 scs, sc in next sc. Repeat from * across, end with sk 5 scs, sc in last st, turn.

Row 4: Ch 7, sc in ch-3 sp, * ch 5, sc in ch-3 sp. Repeat from * across, turn.

Row 5: (Ch 7, sc in first ch-5 sp) twice, * ch 7, sc in next sp, ch 7, sc in same sp. Repeat from * across, end with ch 4, dc in 4th ch of first ch-7 loop in row below, turn.

Row 6: * Ch 7, 5 dc in next ch-7 sp, ch 7, sc in next sp. Repeat from * across, end with ch 4, dc in last ch-7 sp, turn.

Row 7: Ch 3, 4 dc in first ch-7 sp, * ch 3, sc in center of dc of 5-dc group, ch 3, (5 dc in next ch-7 sp) twice. Repeat from * across, end with ch 3, sc in center dc of group, ch 3, 5 dc in last ch-7 sp, turn.

Row 8: Ch 3, sc in center of 5-dc group, ch 3, sc in last dc of same group, * (ch 3, sc, in next sp) twice, ch 3, sc in first dc of next 5-dc group, ch 3, sc in center dc of same group, ch 3, sc between the 5-dc groups, ch 3, sc in center dc of next group, ch 3, sc in last dc of same group. Repeat from * across.

Pink Flower Squares: (use size 10 hook) Ch 6, join with sl st to form a circle.

Rnd 1: Ch 1, sc in center of circle, work (3 dc, sc) 8 times in center of circle, end with sl st in sc. (8 petals made)

Children seem to go from infants to toddlers overnight. To savor the precious time, bundle up baby and enjoy the outdoors. Single crocheted motifs are easily sewn into this washable douvet for baby.

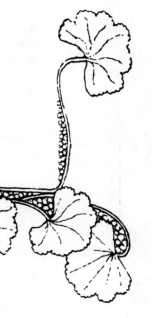

Rnd 2: (Ch 3, sc in back of work between next 2 petals in row below) repeat around, end with sl st in first ch (ch loop made).

Rnd 3: Work (sc, 5 dc) in each ch loop around, end with sl st in first sc. (8 petals made).

Rnd 4: (Ch 4, sc in back between next 2 petals of row below) around. End with sl st in first ch.

Rnd 5: Work (sc, 6 dc) in each loop around, end with sl st in first sc. (8 petals made)

Rnd 6: (Ch 5, sc in back of work between next 2 petals of row below) around. End with sl st in first ch.

Rnd 7: Work (sc, 7 dc) in each ch loop around, end with sl st in first sc. (8 petals made)

Rnd 8: Repeat rnd 6, except ch 6 between sc.

Rnd 9: Repeat rnd 7, except 8 dc in each loop. (8 petals made)

3 Corner Leaves: Attach green thread with sl st in any petal between the sc and first dc, * ch 10, dc in 4th ch from hook, dc in next 2 chs, ch 4, sc in same place as thread was attached. Repeat from * twice. Fasten off. [Sk 2 petals, work 3 corner leaves between sc and first dc of next petal]. Repeat twice.

Rnd 1: Attach white thread in point of center green leaf of any 3-leaf group. (Ch 3, dc, ch 3, 2 dc) in same place, ch 8, 2 dc in point of next leaf, * ch 8, 2 dtrc (thread over hook, 3 times) between sc and first dc of sk sp between petals of flower. Ch 8, 2 dc in point of first leaf of next group, ch 8, (2 dc, ch 3, 2 dc) in point of center leaf, ch 8, 2 dc in point of 3rd leaf of group. Repeat from * twice, to beg corner, end with sl st in top of ch 3.

Rnd 2: Sl st to center of corner ch-3 sp, work (ch 3, dc, ch 3, 2 dc) in ch-3 sp, * 7 dc in next ch-8 sp, dc between 2 dc in point of leaf, 7 dc in next ch-8 sp, dc between 2 dc of point of leaf, 7 dc in next ch-8 sp, 2 dc, ch 3, 2 dc in corner ch-3 sp. Repeat from * around, end with sl st in top of beg ch 3, sl st to ch-3 corner sp.

Rnd 3: Ch 3, (dc, ch 3, 2 dc) in same sp, sk 2 dc, dc between next 2 dc, 32 dc between corner shells.

Rnd 4: Repeat rnd 3, except work 33 dc between corner shells.

Rnd 5: Repeat rnd 3, except work 34 dc between corner shells.

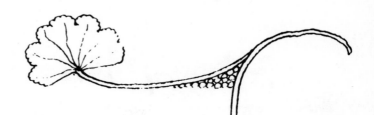

MATERIALS:

118" of crocheted edging
Sixteen crocheted rose blocks
4 yards of pink fabric; matching thread
One infant comforter approximately 28" × 34"
Seven 3/8" white buttons;
  matching thread
Five yards of 1/4"-wide white
  satin ribbon

DIRECTIONS:

All seams are 1/4".

1. Cut two 28" × 34" pieces and one 28" × 6" piece from pink fabric. Also cut 7½" wide strips to measure 8 yards for the ruffle.

2. Stitch all 7½" wide strips together to make one continu-ous piece. Fold wrong sides together to become 3¾" wide. Press. Fold into fourths and mark. Stitch gathering threads along raw edge.

3. Mark the centers of each edge of one 28" × 34" piece for top. Match marks on ruffle piece to centers of top piece, aligning raw edges and placing folded edge of ruffle piece toward center of top. Gather ruffle to fit top, allowing extra at each corner. Stitch.

4. Stitch 1" deep hem on one 28" wide edge of both remain-ing pieces for the back. Make seven buttonholes in the hem of smaller piece (Diagram 1).

5. Fold the douvet top into quarters (Diagram 2). Mark the fold lines. Place the rose blocks on the douvet top (Diagram 3). Slipstitch.

6. Place the douvet top on a flat surface with the ruffle folded toward the center. Place the smaller back piece at top over the douvet top, right sides together, matching raw edges. Place the larger back piece over the first (Diagram 4). Stitch all edges. Trim the corners. Turn.

7. Mark the placement for the buttons. Sew the buttons on.

8. Pin the edging on the dou-vet top, over the seam joining the ruffle and the top. Slip-stitch the edging. Lace the ribbon through the beading, leaving 18" length at the begin-ning and at the end. Tie into a knot, then a bow.

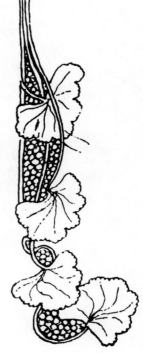

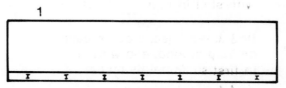

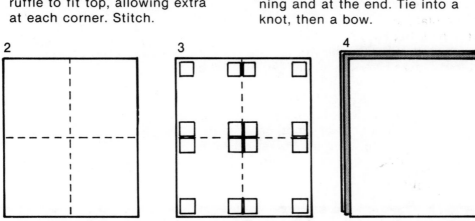

Floral Fan

The floral patterns of yesteryear are etched forever in our minds as we imagine these very fans being displayed above Queen Victoria's very own brass bed.

MATERIALS:
Cebelia #30 White - 1 ball (563 yards per ball)
Cebelia #30 Ivory - 1 ball (563 yards per ball)
1 ply Tandoori Tussah - (400 yards)
Size 7 steel crochet hook
Beads (amber and copper colored)
10" of ¼"–wide flat lace

Using Ivory Cebelia, make 5 roses as for "**A Bridal Basket**", Rows 1 through 8.   Four roses will be sewn on top of crochet when it is completed (one over each shell section). The fifth rose will have 2 rows of White Cebelia worked around as for rose in same pattern working rows 9 and 10. Fasten off. With Tandoori Tussah:

Row 1: Sl st between 2 picots at center of any outside loop of 5th rose, (ch 5, sl st between 2 picots of next loop) 11 times, turn.

Row 2: Ch 4, (7 trc in next ch 5 loop) 11 times.

Row 3: (Beading row) Ch 12, sk 7 trc, trc in next trc, (ch 5, sk 4 trc, trc in next trc) 12 times, ch 9, sk 6 trc, trc in last trc, turn.

Row 4: Ch 1, (sc, hdc, 5 dc, hdc, sc) in next sp, (sc, hdc, 3 dc, hdc, sc) in next sp, 12 times (sc, hdc, 5 dc, hdc, sc) in last sp, turn.

Row 5: * Ch 6, sl st in 3rd st from hook for picot, ch 8, sl st in 3rd ch for picot, ch 3, sc in sc between shells, repeat from * across, end with sc in last st.

Row 6: (Ch 8, sl st in 3rd st from hook for picot) twice, ch 3, sc in center of next loop, * ch 6, sl st for picot in 3rd ch, ch 8, sl st for picot in 3rd ch, ch 3, sc in center of next loop, repeat from * across, end with trc in sc at end of previous row (15 loops), turn.

Row 7: Repeat Row 6 (16 loops).

Rows 8-9: Sl st to center of next loop, repeat between *'s of Row 6, end with trc in sc at end of row, 2 rows below, turn.

Row 10: Ch 11, dc in center of first loop, (ch 8 dc in next loop) across, end with ch 8, trc in beg ch, 2 rows below (17 loops).

Row 11: Ch 1, (sc, 5 dc, sc, 5 dc) in next sp, sc over dc, * (5 dc, sc, 5 dc) in next sp, sc over dc, repeat from * across, end with sc in 5th ch of row below. Do not fasten off.

Edging: Working down side edge, (ch 6, picot in 3rd ch from hook, ch 3, sc in next sp) 5 times, end with sc in side of last dc. Fasten off. Work other side of fan to correspond, making 5 single picot loops. Fasten off. Sew completed roses evenly spaced across fan as shown. Weave lace through beading row securing ends.

A Crochet Bouquet

MATERIALS:

One 6″ × 9½″ piece of cream linen fabric cut on the bias; matching thread

1 ply Tandoori Tussah Thread 1,000 yards

Size –7 steel hook

Dressmaker's pen

Linen Fabric:

1. Mark the intervals on the fabric as shown in the diagram. Along top edge, make a ¼″ deep fold at each mark. Along bottom edge, fold ½″ deep or more until edge is about 2¾″ wide. Baste and press.

2. Place the pattern over the folded linen. Cut basket shape.

3. Hemstitch around outside edge of fabric, going through all layers of fabric at folds. Also make two parallel rows of hemstitching ¼″ apart, 1¾″ and 2″ above bottom edge and again 4″ and 4¼″ above bottom edge.

4. Sc around entire piece. To make center bands, thread hook down through bottom hole and up through top hole of hemstitching. Then sc through both hemstitch rows across center of linen basket. Pull ridge of sc to top.

Large Motifs:

Make 7 motifs; joining as you go.

Rnd 1: Wrap thread around little finger 6 times to form a circle, work 12 sc loosely over the circle.

Rnd 2: (Ch 6, sl st in 3rd ch from hook to make a picot, ch 3, sk 1 sc, sc in next sc) repeat around, end with sl st in beg ch, turn, sl st in next 2 scs, turn (6 loops).

Rnd 3: (Ch 8, sl st in 2nd sc past picot) around, end with ch 4, trc in beg ch (place a safety pin here as a marker).

Rnd 4: Ch 8, sc in next loop, * ch 2, 7 dc in same loop, ch 2, sc in same loop, (ch 8, sc in next loop) twice. Repeat from * twice, omitting last ch-8 loop, sl st in beg ch (where pin was placed).

Rnd 5: 8 Sc in first loop, sc in ch-2 sp, ch 4, * dc in 4th dc of dc group, ch 6, dc in next sc, (ch 6, dc in next loop, ch 6, dc in next sc) twice, ch 6, repeat from * once, end dc in 4th dc of group, ch 4, sc in ch-2 sp, 8 sc in next loop, sl st in beg sc. Fasten off. Second motif will be joined to first on rnd 5 as follows: on last repeat between *s, work only: ch 6, dc in next loop, then ch 3, sl st in corresponding loop of first motif, ch 3, dc in next loop, ch 3, sl st in next loop of first motif, ch 3, dc in next sc, ch 3, sl st in next loop of first motif, ch 3, dc in 4th sc of group, ch 4, sc in ch-2 sp, 8 sc in next loop, sl st in beg sc. Fasten off. Add each of next 6 motifs in same manner.

(continued)

Center Picot Motif:

Make 1 picot motif for center bottom: wind thread around little finger 6 times, slip off carefully to create a circle.

Rnd 1: Ch 3, 20 dc in circle.

Rnd 2: Ch 3, work in back loop only, dc in next 2 dcs, * ch 3, dc in next 3 dcs, repeat from * around, end with ch 3, sl st in top of beg ch (7 sections), turn.

Rnd 3: Sl st in center of ch 3, turn, * ch 8, sl st in 5th ch from hook, picot made, ch 4, sl st in ch-3 loop, repeat from * around, end with sl st in beg ch.

Rnd 4: Sl st in next 3 sts, * ch 8, picot in 5th ch, ch 4, sl st just past picot of previous rnd, ch 8, picot, ch 4, sl st in next loop, just before picot of previous rnd, repeat from * around, end with sl st in beg ch. Fasten off. Set aside.

Small Picot Motifs:

Make 2 motifs: work 2 rnds same as motif above, work 3 picot loops of rnd 3, place motif between last 2 flower motifs on either end of 7 connected motifs. Join as follows: ch 4, sc in 4th sc of 8-sc loop, ch 4, sl st in ch-3 sp of picot motif, ch 4, sc in next loop of flower motif, ch 4, sl st in ch-3 sp of picot motif, ch 4, sc in loop just before 8 sc loop of next flower motif, ch 4, sl st in next ch-3 sp of picot motif, ch 4, sc in 4th ch of 8 sc loop, ch 4, sl st in beg ch of picot motif. Fasten off. Attach second motif to other end of 7 flower motifs.

Arrange motifs around linen fan (see photo). Sew in place with matching thread. Sew the center picot motif below the lower band of sc. To work outside edge of fan, join crochet thread at base of center picot of small picot motif.

Edge:

Row 1: Ch 8, sc in next loop of small picot motif, ch 8, sc in next loop just before picot, ch 8, sc in same loop just beyond picot, ch 8, sc in joining of motifs, (ch 8, sc in next loop) 11 times, ch 8, sc in joining, * (ch 8, sc in next loop) 3 times, ch 8, sc in next dc (center of motif), (ch 8, sc in next loop) 3 times, ch 8, sc in joining, repeat from * 4 more times, (ch 8, sc in next loop) 11 times, ch 8, sc in joining, ch 8, sc in next loop of small motif, just before picot, ch 8, sc in same loop just beyond picot, ch 8, sc in next loop, ch 8, sc at base of picot which is attached to linen, turn.

Row 2: * 8 Sc in first loop, 4 sc in next loop, ch 8, turn, sc in 4th sc of loop just completed, turn, (1 sc, ch 4 make picot by sl st in first ch, 3 sc, picot, 3 sc, picot, 1 sc) in loop just formed, complete 4 sc in unfinished loop, repeat from * around, end with sl st in beg ch of loop.

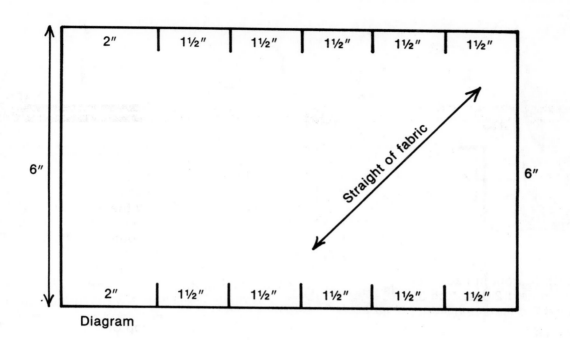

| 2″ | 1½″ | 1½″ | 1½″ | 1½″ | 1½″ |

6″   6″

Straight of fabric

| 2″ | 1½″ | 1½″ | 1½″ | 1½″ | 1½″ |

Diagram

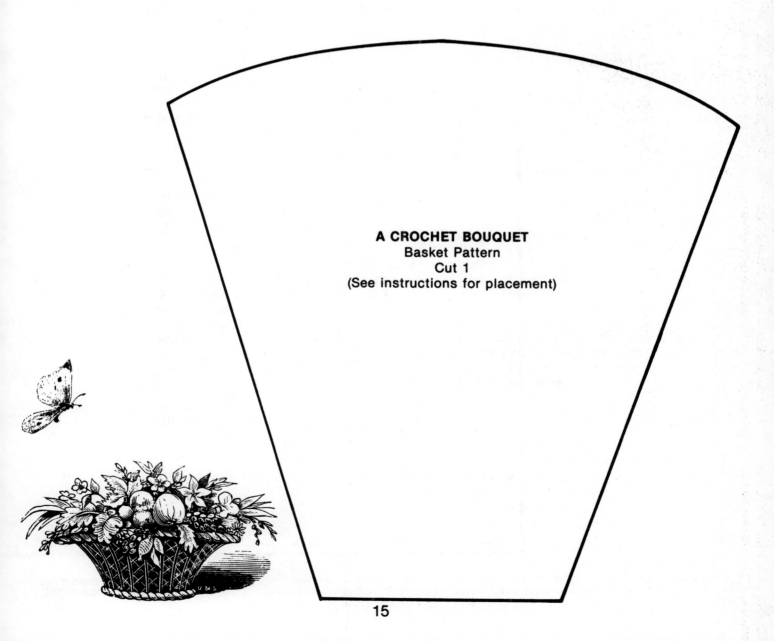

A CROCHET BOUQUET
Basket Pattern
Cut 1
(See instructions for placement)

15

A Cozy Coverlet

Add a touch of drama to your bed spread with this crocheted cover and pillow edge. The cream color will intermingle with any color to form a subtle pattern.

MATERIALS:
Knit Crosheen Cream
Bedspread - 38 balls
(280 yards per ball)
Pillow - 3 balls
(280 yards per ball)
Size 4 steel hook

GAUGE:
3 rows dc = 1″
9 dc = 1″

Large Motif: Make 132 for double bed spread and 12 for standard pillow. Ch 6, join with sl st to form circle.

Rnd 1: Ch 3, 15 dc in circle, sl st to join.

Rnd 2: Ch 4, to create a chain stitch ridge you must work behind each dc of rnd just finished. Work through each bar and one other thread, dc through the bar, ch 1, repeat around, end with ch 1, sl st in 3rd ch of beg. Ridge is on the right side.

Rnd 3: Ch 4, sk 1 st, work a shell of * (2 dc, ch 3, 2 dc) in next dc, ch 1, dc over next dc, ch 1, repeat from * around, end with ch 1, sl st in 3rd ch of beg ch (8 shells).

Rnd 4: Ch 5, work a shell of * (3 dc, ch 4, 3 dc) in ch-4 sp, ch 2, dc over dc, ch 2, repeat from * around, end with ch 2, sl st in 3rd ch of beg ch.

Rnd 5: Ch 6, work a shell of * (4 dc, ch 5, 4 dc) in ch-4 sp, ch 3, dc over dc, ch 3, repeat from * around, end with ch 3, sl st in 3rd ch of beg ch.

Rnd 6: Ch 6, work a shell of * (4 dc, ch 6, 4 dc) in next ch sp, ch 3, dc over dc, ch 3, repeat from * around, end with ch 3, sl st in 3rd ch of beg ch.

Rnd 7: Ch 7, work a shell of * (5 dc, ch 6, 5 dc) in next ch sp, ch 4, dc over dc, ch 4, repeat from * around, end with sl st in 3rd ch of beg ch.

Rnd 8: Ch 8, work a shell of * (6 dc, ch 7, 6 dc) in next ch sp, ch 5, dc over dc, ch 5, repeat from * around, end with sl st in 3rd ch.

Rnd 9: Ch 9, work a shell of * (7 dc, ch 5, 7dc) in next ch sp, ch 6, dc over dc, ch 6, repeat from * around, end with sl st in 3rd ch. Fasten off.

Second Motif: Work to last 2 points, join to any point of 1st motif working * 7 dc, ch 2, sc through point ch-5 of first motif, ch 2, 7 dc in same sp on second motif, ch 6, dc in next dc, dc over dc on first motif, ch 6, repeat from *, end with ch 6, sl st in 3rd ch of beg.

Small Motif: Work same as large motif for 4 rnds. Make 110 small motifs for bed spread and 6 for pillow.

Rnd 5: Join to large motifs. Ch 3, dc in last dc of 7-dc of large

16

motif, ch 3, 3 dc, ch 2 in ch sp of small motif, sc in top of dc of large motif, ch 2, 4 dc in same sp of small motif, ch 3, dc over dc, dc in first of 7-dc of large motif, ch 3, 4 dc in next ch sp of small motif, ch 2, * sc through point ch joining of 2nd large motif, ch 2, 4 dc in same ch sp of small motif, ch 3, dc over dc of small motif, dc in last dc of 7-dc of the new large motif, ch 3, 4 dc in ch sp of small motif, ch 2, sc in dc of the 2nd large motif, ch 2, 4 dc in same sp of small motif, ch 3, dc over next dc, dc in first dc of 7-dc of 2nd large motif, ch 3, 4 dc in next sp of small motif, ch 2, repeat from *, until small motif is connected to 4 large motifs.

Bed Spread Edging:

Rnd 1: Attach thread at joining of corner motif. Working around this corner motif, ch 10, dc in last dc of next dc group, ch 7, dc over next dc, ch 7, dc in first dc of next dc group, ch 7, 6 dc in ch loop at point, ch 7, dc in last dc of dc group, ch 7, dc over next dc, ch 7, dc in first dc of next dc group, ch 7, 6 dc in point. Continue in same manner around, end with sl st in top of beg ch.

Note: Work only 1 dc in joining of motifs.

Rnd 2: Ch 3, * (6 dc in next sp, dc over next dc) 4 times, work 1 dc over next 6 dc at point, repeat from *, continue in same manner around, end with sl st in top of turning ch.

Rnd 3: Ch 4, sk 1 st, work a three trc cluster in next st as follows: thread over hook twice, (thread over and pull through 2 loops) twice, hold back last loop of each trc, as before, work 2 more trc in same sp, thread over and pull through all 4 loops on hook, ch 5, sk across to next dc over dc, work cluster in this dc, ch 5, sk to next dc over dc, work cluster in this dc, ch 5, cluster in next dc, * sk to next dc over dc, ch 5, cluster in this dc, sk to first dc of 6 dc group at point, cluster in this dc, ch 5, cluster in center dc of same group, ch 5, cluster in last dc of same group, (sk to next dc over dc, cluster in this dc, ch 5) twice, cluster in next dc, repeat from * 3 times, ch 5, cluster in next dc over dc, ch 5, sk 4 dcs, cluster in next dc, sk 1, trc over next dc over dc, (this is directly above the joining of motifs), sk 1 dc, cluster in next dc, ch 5, sk to next dc over dc, cluster in this dc, ch 5, sk to next dc over dc, cluster in this dc, ch 5, cluster in next dc, repeat between *'s twice, ch 5, sk to next dc over dc, cluster in next dc, ch 5, sk 4 sts, cluster in next dc, trc over next dc over dc overjoining. Continue in this manner around bed spread.

17

Pillow Cover Edge

Join twelve large motifs and six motifs in same pattern as for coverlet. Crochet edge on one short end.

Row 1: Work same as bed spread edge beginning at one short side 2 points before joining, ch 10, * dc in last dc of dc group, ch 7, dc over next dc, ch 7, dc in first dc of dc group, ch 7, 6 dc in point loop, ch 7, dc over last dc of dc group, ch 7, dc over next dc, ch 7, dc over first dc of dc group, ch 7, * dc in joining of 2 motifs, ch 7, repeat between *'s, 6 dc in point loop. Work in same manner to second point loop of 3rd motif of short end, dc in point loop, ch 3, turn.

Row 2: (Work 6 dc in next sp, dc over dc) 3 times, * 6 dc in next sp, dc over next 6 dc at point, * repeat between () 7 times, then repeat between * once, repeat from beg of row, end, repeat between () 4 times, from ch 4, turn.

Row 3: Work as rnd 3 of bed spread edge.

Center crocheted piece over standard size cream pillow case. Fold excess to back side. Slipstitch to pillow case, folding corners smoothly on back side.

Keepsake Box

MATERIALS:
Cebelia #30 Ivory - 1 ball (563 yards per ball)
Size 8 steel hook
GAUGE: 4 Rows dc = 1″
20 dc = 1″

Row 1: Ch 10, turn, sk 1 st, dc in next 2 sts, picot of ch 3, sl st in first ch, dc in next 5 sts, picot, dc in next 2 sts, ch 8, turn.

Row 2: Sl st in center dc of 5 dc group, turn.

Row 3: Ch 3, 8 dc in loop, ch 4, turn.

Row 4: Sk 2 dcs, dc in next dc, (ch 2, dc in next dc) 5 times, (there should be 6 sps), ch 7, sl st in top of end dc of first row, turn.

Row 5: [Ch 3, 2 dc, (picot, 3 dc) twice, picot, 2 dc], all in next sp, [(1 dc, picot, 2 dc) in next sp, 3 dc in next sp] twice, (1 dc, picot, 2 dc) in next sp, 2 dc in last sp, ch 8, turn.

Row 6: Sk to first st beyond first picot, sl st in this st, turn.

Row 7: Ch 3, 8 dc in loop, ch 4, turn.

Row 8: Sk 3 dcs, dc in next dc, (ch 2, dc in next dc) 5 times, ch 7, sk across to center st of 3-dc group just beyond the first picot, sl st in this center st, turn. Repeat rows 5 through 8 for pattern to desired length, turn, work along the long top edge of trim as follows: ch 3, (3 dc, picot) in each row, end: 3 dc in last row, dc in beg ch of trim. Fasten off.

Close to the heart of a woman are places for the safekeeping of precious objects. The parts for making our floral box were found at a local craft store and we added our own trim. The feminine lace collar shown in the photo (page 36) may be either worn to dress up your favorite silken blouse or framed as a decorative piece of art.

Lace Collar

MATERIALS:
Cordonnet #30 Ecru - 2 balls
  (216 yds per ball)
Size 10 steel hook
1¼ yards ⅛″–wide ribbon
323 small pearl beads

GAUGE: 12 dc = 1″
        4 rows dc = 1″

Row 1: Ch 204, sc in second ch and each ch across.

Row 2: (Beading) Ch 3, dc in next st, (ch 1, sk 1 st, dc in next st) across, end with dc in last st, turn.

Row 3: Ch 1, sc in each st across, turn.

Row 4: Ch 1, sc in same st, (ch 5, sk 2 scs, sc in next sc) across, end with sc in last sc, turn.

Row 5: Ch 7, (sc in next loop, ch 5) across, end with sc in last loop, turn.

Row 6: Ch 8, sc in next loop, (ch 6, sc in next loop) across, turn.

Row 7: Ch 8, (sc in next loop, ch 6) across, end with sc in last loop, turn.

Row 8: Ch 9, (sc in next loop, ch 7) across, end with sc in last loop, turn.

Row 9: Repeat row 8. Set aside to be joined to medallions later (bottom edge). Make medallions as follows:

First medallion:

Rnd 1: Ch 4, sl st to form a circle, ch 1, 11 sc in circle, end with sl st in ch 1.

Rnd 2: Ch 3, 23 dc in circle, end with sl st in top of beg ch.

Rnd 3: Ch 1, sc in same place (ch 6, sk 2 dcs, sc in next dc) 8 times, except end with sl st in beg sc.

Rnd 4: Work 7 sc in each sp around, end with sl st in beg sc.

Rnd 5: Ch 1, sc in same place, (ch 5, sk 3 scs, sc in next - center - sc, ch 5, sk 3 scs, sc between next 2 sc) around, end with sl st in beg sc.

Rnd 6: Ch 1, sc in same place, (3 sc, ch 3, sl st in ch-1 for picot, 3 sc in next sp) around, end with sl st in beg sc.

Rnd 7: (Joining rnd) ch 1, sc in same place, (ch 7, st in center sc between picots 11 times. Join to the collar section which was set aside earlier, as follows: ch 3, (join to bottom edge of collar section, holding beading row at top, dc in first loop on right hand edge of row

9 of collar section) ch 3, sc between next 2 picots of medallion, (ch 3, sc in next loop of collar, ch 3, sc between next 2 picots of medallion) 3 times, ch 3, dc in next loop of collar, ch 3, sl st in beg sc. Fasten off. Medallions will be joined together as they are attached to the collar section.

Second Medallion: Work next collar medallion through Rnd 6. Work as Rnd 7 directions until 8 loops are worked. Ch 3, sc in 3rd loop made on first medallion (rnd 7), ch 3, (sc between next 2 picots of second medallion. Ch 3, sc in next loop of first medallion twice, ch 3, sc between next 2 picots of second medallion, ch 3, dc in next loop of first medallion, dc in same loop of collar that the last dc was worked, (ch 3, sc between next 2 picots of second medallion, ch 3, sc in next loop of collar) 3 times, ch 3, sc between next 2 picots of second medallion, ch 3, dc in next loop of collar, ch 3, sc in beg sc. Fasten off. Make other medallions and join them together and to collar section in same way (16 medallions). Do not fasten off on last joining, sl st to center of next loop.

Bottom Edge:

Row 1: (Ch 7, sc in next loop) 7 times, * ch 7, sc in joining where 2 medallions meet, (ch 7, sc in next loop) 5 times, repeat from * across. Continue up side edge of collar working ch 7, sc in next loop to beading, ch 3, sc in top corner edge of collar, continue across top edge, ch 7, sk 5 sts, sc in next st, continue down other side edge, ch 3, sc in bottom of beading row, ch 7, sc in next loop, end with sl st in beg ch of rnd. Fasten off.

Row 2: With right side of medallion facing you, work across bottom. Attach thread to 5th loop from first joining. Work 4 sc, picot, 4 sc in each loop across bottom edge of collar, end working 5 loops of last medallion. Fasten off.

Top Edge: With right side facing you, work same as bottom edge, 4 sc, picot, 4 sc in each loop. Fasten off. Lace ribbon through beading row.

Sew beads onto medallions as follows:

Using same color thread, sew one bead onto each picot of rnd 6. (16 beads per medallion, 256 total) Sew beads on beading row of collar, at the bottom of every other dc. (67 beads)

Floral Bed Cover

Borrowed from Old
Europe, the douvet or
bed cover is today a
part of everyday
American life.
Whether placed upon
an antique family bed
or one more contem-
porary, this floral
cover with its
crocheted borders is
both inviting and
practical. Add piles
of soft pillows and
the promise of a
warm restful nights
sleep will surely be
kept.

SIZE: Double bed

MATERIALS:
Wondersheen color 25 Aqua -
  20 skeins (400 yds per skein)
Size 7 steel hook
Size 4 steel hook

GAUGE:
15 dc = 2½"
4 rows dc = 2½"

Aqua Comforter Edge:
10 large motifs
110 small motifs (25 for
elaborate crochet end, 25 for
other short end and 30 for
each side)
11 tiny motifs
204 rows of insertion pattern

Aqua Pillow Edge: (for each pillow)
3 large motifs
7 small motifs
4 tiny motifs
58 rows of insertion pattern

Large Motif: (size 7 hook) Each
large motif is 8″ in diameter.
Ch 6, sl st to form a circle.

Rnd 1: Ch 3, 11 dc in circle, sl
st to close in top of beg ch 3.

Rnd 2: Ch 6, (dc in next dc, ch
3), around, end with sl st in 3rd
ch of beg ch, sl st in next sp
(12 sps).

Rnd 3: Ch 3, 4 dc in same sp,
ch 5, sk 1 sp, (5 dc in next sp,
ch 5, sk 1 sp) around, end with
sl st in top of turning ch.

Rnd 4: Ch 3, dc in each of next
4 dc, (5 dc in ch-5 sp, dc in
each of next 5 dc) around, end
with 5 dc in last sp, sl st in
top of turning ch.

Rnd 5: Ch 3, dc in each of next
4 dc, (ch 5, sk 2 dcs, dc in next
dc, ch 5, sk 2 dcs, dc in each
of next 5 dcs) around, end with
ch 5, sk 2 dcs, dc in next dc,
ch 5, sl st in top of beg ch.

Rnd 6: Ch 3, holding back last
loop of each dc, dc in each of
next 4 dcs, thread over and
pull through all 5 loops on
hook, * (ch 6, dc in next dc)
twice, ch 6, holding back last
loop of each dc, dc in each of
next 5 dcs, (cluster made),
thread over and pull through 6
loops on hook, repeat from *
around, end with (ch 6, dc in
next dc) twice, ch 6, sl st in
top of beg ch.

Rnd 7: Ch 8, dc in next sp (ch
5, dc in next sp) twice, * ch 5,
dc in ch-1 closure at point of
cluster, (ch 5, dc in next sp) 3
times, repeat from * around,
end with ch 5, sl st in 3rd ch
of beg ch (24 sps).

Rnd 8: Ch 3, 2 dc in same
place as sl st, * ch 3, sc in
next sp, (ch 8, sc in next sp) 3
times, ch 3, work 5 dc in next
dc above point of cluster,
repeat from * around, end with
working 2 dc in same place as
beg ch.

Rnd 9: Ch 5, trc in next dc, ch 1, trc in next dc, * ch 3, sc in next ch-8 sp (ch 8, sc in next sp) twice, ch 3, (trc in next dc, ch 1) 4 times, trc in next dc, ch 3, repeat from * around, end with trc in 1st dc of section where you began, ch 1, trc in next dc, ch 1, sl st in 4th ch.

Rnd 10: Make a starting popcorn as follows: ch 4, 3 trc in same place as sl st, drop loop on hook and insert hook through top of beg ch 4 and pull dropped loop through. Note: make all other popcorns with 4 trc - (ch 2, popcorn in next trc) twice, * ch 5, sc in next ch-8 sp, ch 9, sc in next ch-8 sp, ch 5, popcorn in next trc, (ch 2, popcorn in next trc) 4 times, repeat from * around, end with popcorn over first trc of section where you began, ch 2, popcorn in next trc, ch 2, sl st in top of beg popcorn.

Rnd 11: (Sc in next sp between popcorn, ch 5, popcorn in same sp, ch 3, sl st in top of popcorn to make a picot, ch 5, sc in same sp), repeat between () once except omit last sc, * (work 6 sc, ch 4, 6 sc), in next ch-8 sp, ch 5, (work popcorn, ch 3, picot, ch 5) in next sp between popcorn, sc in same sp, repeat between () 3 times except omit last sc. Repeat from * around, except end with repeat between () once, sl st in beg sc. Other motifs are joined with sl st in 2 popcorns, sl st to ch-4 between the 6-sc groups, sl st in 2 popcorns.

Small motif: Each small motif is 3″ in diameter. Ch 3, dc in first ch to form a circle.

Rnd 1: Ch 3, 11 dc in circle, sl st in top of beg ch.

Rnd 2: Ch 8, (sk 1 dc, dc in next dc, ch 5) around, end with sl st in 3rd ch of beg ch (6 sps).

Rnd 3: Ch 3, (7 dc in next sp, dc over dc) around, end with 7 dc in last sp, sl st in top of beg ch.

Rnd 4: Ch 1, sc in same place, (ch 5, sk 3 dc, sc in next dc) around, end with sl st in beg sc (12 loops).

Rnd 5: Ch 2, (7 dc in next sp, hdc in sc) around, end with sl st in top of beg ch.

Joining motifs together - second small motif:

Make second motif, joining to first motif on last rnd. Work as for first motif except when working in the last 2 loops, * 4 dc, sl st in center st of corresponding section of last motif, work 3 more dc in same loop of present motif, hdc in next st, repeat from * in next loop. Fasten off.

Tiny motif: Each motif is 2″ in diameter.
Ch 6, sl st to form a circle.

Rnd 1: Ch 3, work 23 dc in circle, end with sl st in top of beg ch.

Rnd 2: Ch 6, sk 1 dc, dc in next dc, (ch 3, sk 1 dc, dc in next dc) 10 times, end with ch 3, sl st in 3rd ch of beg ch (12 sps).

Rnd 3: Sc in same place, (ch 6, sc in next dc) around, end with ch 3, sl st in beg sc (12 loops).

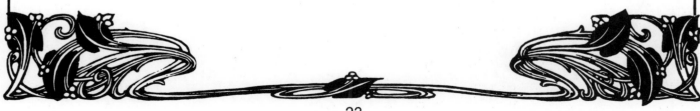

Insert for Comforter and Pillow edge:

Ch 28, turn.

Row 1: Sc in 17th ch from hook, (ch 7, sk 3, sc in next st) 3 times, ch 10, turn.

Row 2: Sc in next loop, ch 7, sc in next loop, ch 5, 5 dc in next loop, ch 5, sc in next loop, ch 13, turn.

Row 3: Sc in ch-5 loop, (ch 7, sc in next loop) 3 times, ch 10, turn.

Row 4: Sc in first loop, ch 5, 5 dc in next loop, ch 5, sc in next loop, ch 7, sc in next loop, ch 13, turn.

Row 5: Sc in first loop, (ch 7, sc in next loop) 3 times, ch 10, turn. Repeat Rows 2 through 5 for pattern - 50 times. 72" (same length as 10 large motifs or 25 small motifs joined in a row. End with row 4 of pattern then work a finishing row of ch 4, sc in each loop across.

Border: Working around the insertion, ch 3, 2 dc in same place, turning corner and working down long side: (3 dc in next sp, dc in sc) to corner, 5 dc in corner st, work across short end, down other long side and other short end, work 2 dc in same place as beg ch (corner) sl st to top of beg ch. Leave thread attached and assemble tiny motifs to this insertion as directed.

Setting tiny motifs together with insertion:
Right sides facing, work along the long side of insertion. Fasten thread to corner of insertion, * ch 3, dc in any loop of tiny motif, ch 3, sk 3 dcs of insertion, sc in dc (ch 3, sc in next loop of tiny motif, ch 3, sk 3 dcs, sc in next dc of insertion) twice, ch 3, dc in next loop of tiny motif, (ch 6, sk 3 sts of insertion, sc in next dc) 6 times, repeat from * adding a new tiny motif as you work across row. Fasten off.

Note: for pillow - sk only 2 dcs of insertion between ch 6, sc in next dc (6 times).

Setting large motif section together with insertion:

Note: Cluster will be referred to as cl

Join thread to 5th unworked loop of tiny motif on outside edge, sc in same sp, then sc in the 2nd cl of second unworked cl group from joining of large motifs, * ch 5, sc in next cl, sc in next loop of tiny motif, ch 5, dc in next loop of tiny motif, dc in 3rd sc of large motif, trc in next loop of tiny motif, dtrc in joining of insertion and tiny motif, sc in picot of large motif, trc in next loop of insertion, dc in 3rd sc of large motif, ch 5, dc in next cl of large motif, trc in next loop of insertion, ch 6, dc in next loop of insertion, dc in next cl, ch 5, dc in next cl, dc in next loop of insertion, ch 6, trc in next loop of insertion, dc in cl of large motif, ch 6, dc in 3rd sc of large motif, trc in next loop

of insertion, sc in picot loop of large motif, dtrc in joining of tiny motif and insertion, trc in next loop of tiny motif, dc in 3rd sc of large motif, dc in next loop of tiny motif, ch 6, dc in next cl of large motif, dc in next loop of tiny motif, ch 6, sc in next loop of tiny motif, sc in cl of large motif, ch 3, sc in next cl of new large motif, sc in next loop of tiny motif, repeat from * to end of row. Using size 4 hook, work along top edge of assembled crochet section. Setting small motifs together with insertion section: working with 2 strands of thread, attach to corner of insertion, ch 8, trc in center of 4th petal of motif from joining at bottom edge, ch 3, sk 5 dcs of insertion, trc in next dc, ch 5, sk 4 dcs of insertion, trc in next dc, ch 3, sk 2 petals of motif, trc in center of next petal just before the joining, ch 3, sk 4 dcs of insertion, trc in next dc, ch 5, sk 4 dcs of insertion, trc in next dc, ch 3, trc in first petal of motif just beyond the joining, ch 3, sk 4 dcs of insertion, trc in next dc, ch 5, sk 4 dcs of insertion, trc in next dc, ch 3, sk 2 petals of insertion, trc in center of next petal, ch 3, sk 4 dcs of insertion, trc in next dc, ch 5, sk 4 dcs of insertion, trc in next dc. Continue in same manner sk only 3 dcs of insertion every time until there are 2½ motifs left, then sk 4 dcs of insertion 8 times, end with sk 5 dcs, this will bring you to the end of the row.

Note: for pillow case, sk 4 dcs, then sk 3 dcs, (alternating across the row) when working in the insertion

DOUVET

Materials: (for 70″ × 85″ douvet)
10 yards of 55″-wide drapery print fabric
Nine ½″-wide buttons

Directions:
All seam allowances are ½″.

1. Cut fabric into the following pieces:

One 55″ × 85″ piece for center front panel

Two 8½ × 85″ pieces for front side panels

One 55″ × 95″ piece for center back panel

Two 8½″ × 95″ pieces for back side panel

2. Stitch one front side panel to each long edge of the center front panel. Repeat for the back.

3. Cut the back panel 39″ from one 70″-wide end. Stitch a 3″ deep hem in one 70″ end of both back pieces.

4. Mark and stitch nine vertical buttonholes ⅝″-wide in the hem of the smaller piece for the back.

5. Place the front on a flat surface right side up. Matching top 70″ edges, place the smaller back piece over the front with right sides together. Matching bottom 70″ edges, place the larger back piece over the front with right sides together and overlapping the smaller back piece. Stitch around entire edge of douvet.

6. Use one of the following methods or your own to anchor the comforter in the douvet. Some attach with snaps, others have elastic loops on the comforter and need ribons to tie through them from the douvet. Most methods can be attached to the seam allowance inside the douvet.

7. Turn the douvet right side out. Mark placement for buttons to match buttonholes. Sew on buttons.

8. Slipstitch crochet trim to douvet, attaching wide border to seam of top edge and medallion border to side and bottom edges.

9. Insert comforter.

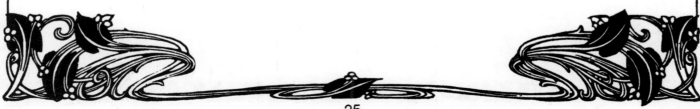

# Table Cloth Tassles

From old to new, we found an old quilt worn on one side and used the other side for a new bedside tablecloth. It was cut into a circle and the edge was hem-stitched. The crocheted border is 12" wide, but can vary depending upon how the fringe is trimmed. The basket pillow is just the right accent with traditional crochet added to the chintz pillow.

MATERIALS:
Cordonnet #30 White - 1 ball
   (216 yards per ball)
Reynolds Saucy White - 8 balls
   (185 yards per ball)
Size 4 steel hook
Size 1 steel hook

GAUGE:
7 (dc, ch-2) sps = 4"

Cordonnet and size 4 hook:
Work 1 sc in each hemstitched hole, sl st in beg sc. Fasten off.

Rnd 1: Attach Saucy, ch 5, * sk 3 scs, dc in next sc, ch 2, repeat from *, end with sl st in 3rd ch of beg ch.

Size 1 hook:

Rnd 2: Sl st into next sp, sc in same sp, * (ch 5, sc in next sp) twice, ch 7, sk 1 sp, sc in next sp, repeat from * around, end with ch 3, trc in beg sc.

Rnd 3: Sc in sp just made, ch 5, sc in next sp, * ch 3, sc in next sp, 11 dc in next ch-7 sp, sc in next sp, ch 3, sc in next sp, (ch 5, sc in next sp) twice, ch 3, sc in next sp (ch 5, sc in next sp) twice, repeat from * around, end with ch 3, dc in beg sc.

Rnd 4: Sc in sp just made, * ch 5, sc in next sp, ch 3, sk next sp, dc in next sc, (ch 3, sl st in first ch, picot made, ch 1, sk 2 dc, dc in next dc) 4 times, ch 3, sc in next sp, ch 3, sc in same sp, ch 3, sc in next sp, repeat from * around, end with ch 3, dc in beg sc.

Rnd 5: [(Ch 5, sc in next sp) twice, * (ch 6, make a picot: sl st in 4th ch from hook) twice, ch 3, sk dc and picot, sc in next dc, repeat from * twice except last sc in ch-3 sp, (ch 5, sc in next sp) twice, ch 3, sc in same sp, ch 5, sc in next sp, ch 3, sc in same sp] repeat around, end with sl st in beg ch.

Rnd 6: Sl st into center of next sp, ch 6, sc in next sp, * (ch 6, sc in next sp between picots) 3 times, (ch 6, sc in next sp) 3 times, ch 3, sc in same sp, (ch 6, sc in next sp) twice, repeat from * around, end with ch 3, trc in beg ch.

Rnd 7: Sc in same sp, (ch 6, sc in next sp) around, end with ch 3, trc in beg sc. Fasten off.

Finishing: Cut fringe 22" long. Place 4 strands together for each fringe and knot in each loop around. Trim length as necessary.

# Crocheted Basket

MATERIALS:
Cordonnet #30 Ecru Natural - 1
ball (216 yards per ball)
Size 10 steel hook

GAUGE:
12 dc = 1″
4 rows dc = 1″

Basket: Ch 25.

Row 1: Skipping 1 ch, sc in each ch across, ch 1, turn.

Row 2: Sc in first 3 sc, dc in next 3 sc. Trc in next 3 sc, dtrc in next 6 sc, trc in next 3 sc, dc in next 3 sc, sc in last 3 sc, ch 2, turn.

Row 3: Skipping first st, dc in each st across, ch 2, turn.

Row 4: 1 Dc in second dc of previous row, ch 1, sk 1 dc, * dc, in next 2 dc, ch 1, sk 1 dc. Repeat from *, end with (1 dc, sk 1 dc, and 1 dc) in loop of ch 2 of previous row. (This row should have seven ch-1 sps), turn, sl st to first ch-1 sp.

Row 5: Ch 2, (1 dc, ch 2, 2 dc) in first ch-1 sp. In each ch-1 space, make shell consisting of 2 dc, ch 1, 2 dc. Turn, sl st to ch-1 sp of first shell.

Row 6: Repeat Row 5.

Row 7: Same as Row 5, except ch 1 between shells.

Row 8: Repeat Row 7.

Row 9: Same as Row 5, except ch 2 between shells.

Row 10: Repeat Row 9.

Row 11: Same as Row 5, except ch 3 between shells.

Row 12: Repeat Row 11.

Row 13: Same as Row 5, except ch 4 between shells.

Row 14: Repeat Row 13, ch 1, turn.

Row 15: Sc in each dc and in each ch of previous row, turn. Sl st in second to last sc of Row 15.

Handle: Ch 2, (1 dc, ch 1, 2 dc) in same sc of Row 15, * turn, sl st to ch-1 sp of shell, ch 2, (1 dc, ch 1, 2 dc) in ch-1 sp of previous shell. Repeat from * until handle measures approximately 8″. Attach with sl st to second to last sc on opposite side of Row 15. Fasten off.

Edging: Beginning at bottom corner, crochet a picot edging consisting of 1 sc, * ch 4, sl st in second stitch of ch 4, ch 1, sc in next stitch along edge. Repeat from * around sides and handle of basket.

Bottom of Basket: Work four evenly spaced shells as in Row 5 across bottom, turn. Next row: [1 sc in first st, ch 2, 1 sc in next stitch.] Repeat across bottom. Fasten off and block.

Basket Pillow

MATERIALS:
Completed crochet basket
⅜ yard of blue chintz fabric; matching thread
¼ yard of yellow chintz fabric
1¼ yards of ¾"-wide yellow satin ribbon; matching thread
½ yard of ⅜"-wide orange grosgrain ribbon; matching thread
1¼ yards of ⅛"-wide olive green satin ribbon
Stuffing
Tracing paper for pattern

DIRECTIONS:
All seams are ¼".

1. Make pattern for pillow.

2. Using pattern, cut two pillow pieces from blue fabric. Cut one 5" × 45" piece for ruffle from yellow fabric.

3. Center crocheted basket over right side of one blue pillow piece 1½" above bottom edge. Slipstitch basket to pillow top. Mark center of top edge of pillow.

4. Fold right sides of ruffle piece together to measure 2½" wide. Stitch short ends. Turn and press. Mark center of raw edge. Stitch gathering threads near raw edge. Gather to 15".

5. Match centers of ruffle and pillow front on raw edges, placing ruffle over pillow front. Pin ends of ruffle ¼" from each corner of top edge. Stitch ruffle to pillow top.

6. Stitch pillow front and back together, keeping ruffle toward center and leaving bottom edge open. Trim corners. Turn. Stuff firmly. Slipstitch opening closed.

7. Make ribbon flowers (see box). From yellow satin ribbon, make five large and five small ribbon flowers, eight orange ribbon flowers, six large looped leaves and three small looped leaves. Pin the flowers in the desired arrangement; see photo. Tack each securely, then add leaves.

8. With remaining green ribbon, knot a loop in one end similar to the large leaf. Thread second end through basket (see photo) and knot again.

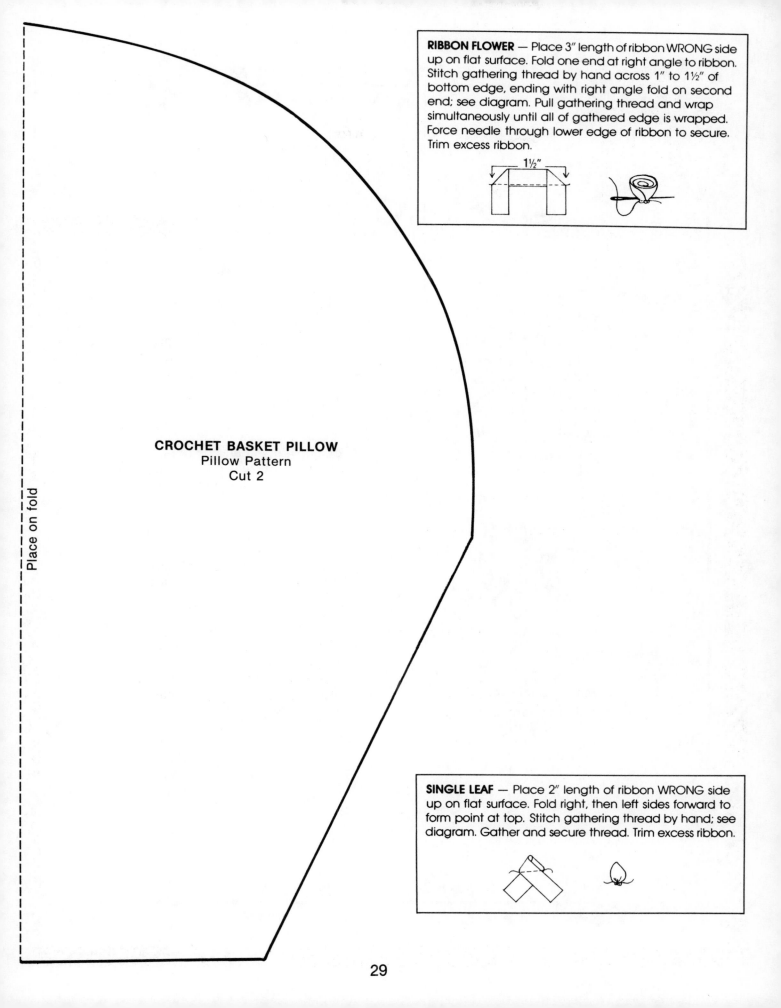

CROCHET BASKET PILLOW
Pillow Pattern
Cut 2

Place on fold

RIBBON FLOWER — Place 3" length of ribbon WRONG side up on flat surface. Fold one end at right angle to ribbon. Stitch gathering thread by hand across 1" to 1½" of bottom edge, ending with right angle fold on second end; see diagram. Pull gathering thread and wrap simultaneously until all of gathered edge is wrapped. Force needle through lower edge of ribbon to secure. Trim excess ribbon.

1½"

SINGLE LEAF — Place 2" length of ribbon WRONG side up on flat surface. Fold right, then left sides forward to form point at top. Stitch gathering thread by hand; see diagram. Gather and secure thread. Trim excess ribbon.

Sun Catcher

This simple sun catcher is made to accent the beauty of light as it passes through the crystal prism. Just use plenty of starch to assure your success.

MATERIALS:

Cordonnet #30 White - 1 ball
    (216 yards per ball)
Size 8 steel hook
1 crystal teardrop

GAUGE:

4 rows dc = 1″
20 dc = 1″

Links: Ch 3, dc in first ch, * ch 3, dc between ch and dc (2 links made). Repeat from * until desired number of links are made. Make 48 ch 3, dc, links. Sl st in first link. Join being careful not to twist.

Rnd 1: Working down the ch 3 side of links, sl st to center of first link, (ch 6, sc in next link) around, end with sl st in beg ch.

Rnd 2: Ch 6, sc in next loop, * ch 3, hold back the last loop of each dc, work 3 dc in sc just made, thread over, pull through all loops, ch 1, - closure -, hold back the last loop of each dc, work 4 dc in the 3rd ch of next loop, thread over, pull thread through all loops, (ch 4, hold back last loop, work 2 dc in the ch 1 - closure - of 1st petal, ch 4, sl st in same place) twice, ch 4, holding back last loop work 3 dc in same place,

(continued)

thread over, pull through all loops, sc in next loop, (ch 6, sc in next loop) twice, repeat from * around, end with ch 3, dc in beg ch (12 flowers).

Rnd 3: Ch 7, sc in next loop, * ch 7, sc in point of first free petal, ch 7, sc in second free petal, (ch 7, sc in next loop) twice, repeat from * around, end with ch 4, trc in beg ch.

Rnd 4: (Ch 7, sc in next loop) around, end with ch 4, trc in beg ch.

Rnd 5: Ch 7, sc in next loop, * ch 6, 2 dc in 3rd ch, ch 3, sl st in same place, (ch 3, 2 dc in same place, ch 3, sl st in same place) twice, ch 3, sc in next loop, (ch 7, sc in next loop) 3 times, repeat from * around, end with ch 4, trc in beg ch.

Rnd 6: Ch 7, sc in next loop, * ch 10, sc in center petal of flower, ch 10, sc in next loop, (ch 7, sc in next loop) twice, repeat from * around, end with ch 4, trc in beg ch.

Rnd 7: Ch 1, 5 sc in loop just made, (5 sc, ch 3, 5 sc) in next loop, * (5 sc, ch 3, 5 sc, ch 3, 5 sc) in next loop, ch 3, (5 sc, ch 3, 5 sc, ch 3, 5 sc) in next loop, (5 sc, ch 3, 5 sc in next loop) twice, repeat from * around, end with 5 sc, ch 3, sl st in beg ch.

Butterfly Center:

Row 1: Leave 2 center ch links open directly under 3 petal flower. Attach thread in next link, ch 9, sl st in 4th ch from hook for picot, ch 10, sl st in 5th ch for picot, ch 9, sl st in 4th ch for picot, ch 5, sk 2 links, sc in next link, ch 3, sc in next link, turn.

Row 2: Ch 7, work a trc cluster in center picot of last row as follows: thread over hook twice, insert hook in center of picot thread over, (pull through 2 loops) twice, hold back last loop of each, work 4 trc in same place, thread over pull through all loops, ch 9 , sl st in 4th ch just made for picot, ch 5, work a dc cluster in same picot as before, holding back last loop of 4 dc, thread over and draw through all loops on hook, ch 9, sl st in 4th ch for picot, ch 5, work 1 more dc cluster in same picot as before, ch 9, sl st in 4th ch for picot, ch 5, work a trc cluster in same picot as before, ch 7, sc in next link of center, ch 3, turn, sl st in beg ch of first row of butterfly. Fasten off. Starch.

See Page 9

See Pages 12 and 13

Pink Afghan

Fifty six medallions blossom out to form this beautiful afghan bursting with color. It is perfect for any season, draped over a chair in the spring or used to stay warm during the first winter's snow fall.

SIZE: 54″ × 64″

MATERIALS:
Brunswick Monterey Yarn - 21 skeins (105 yards per skein)
Size "I" hook

GAUGE:
4 rows dc = 4″
20 dc = 4″

Each medallion is 5″ × 5″. Make afghan medallions, joining them as they are worked. Crochet border around entire afghan. Add border medallions as they are worked. Add flower inserts.

Afghan: Ch 6, sl st to make a circle.

Rnd 1: Ch 3, 19 dc in ring (20). Sl st in 3rd ch at beg.

Rnd 2: Ch 4, (dc, ch 1) in each dc around. Join with sl st in 3rd ch at beg, sl st in first ch-1 sp.

Rnd 3: Ch 3, 2 dc in same sp, (3 dc in next ch-1 sp) 3 times (4 groups) * ch 7, sk 1 sp, (3 dc in next ch-1 sp) 4 times. Repeat from *, end with ch 7, sl st in top of beg ch. Fasten off. Second medallion is attached to the first as follows: work 1 side of rnd 3, ch 3, holding first medallion behind second medallion, wrong sides together, sc through center st of ch-7 corner of first medallion, ch 3, sk 1 sp, * 3 dc in next ch-1 sp of second medallion, sc through first medallion between next two 3-dc groups. Repeat from * twice (attached 3 places), 3 dc in next ch-1 sp (4th group), ch 3, attach corner with sc through center st of ch 7 of first medallion, ch 3, continue around second medallion completing rnd 3. Fasten off. Fasten 8 medallions together in same way making a row.
Now start second row, one medallion at a time. Attach 1st medallion of row 2 underneath end medallion. Attach second medallion to first row and the next medallion of row 2 (two sides joined). Corners of each medallion are joined together: ch 3, sc through center of ch-7 loops. Work in same way until 10 rows of 8 medallions are set together. (80 medallions).

Border:

Rnd 1: Attach yarn to any corner sp ch 3, 3 dc in same sp, *(sk 3 dc, work a shell of 3 dc between 3dc shell of medal-

lions) 3 times, (3 dc shell in next sp) twice, repeat from * to corner, 7 dc in corner sp, continue in same manner around, end with 3 dc in beg sp, sl st in top of beg ch.

Rnd 2: Working loosely, ch 5, *sk 1 dc, dc in next dc, ch 2, sk 1 dc, dc in next sp, (ch 2, dc in center dc of next shell) to corner section, dc in sp just before 7 dc, (ch 2, sk 1 dc, dc in next dc) twice, ch 2, dc in same dc for corner sp, ch 2, repeat from * around end with dc in same place as beg ch, ch 2, sl st in 3rd ch of beg ch. Turn, sl st in sp just made, turn.

Rnd 3: Ch 3, dc, ch 2, 2 dc shell in same sp, *ch 1, (2dc in next sp, ch 1) to corner sp, 2 dc, ch 2, 2 dc in this sp, repeat from * around, end with ch 1, sl st in top of beg ch.

Border Medallions:
First Medallion: Ch 6, sl st to make a ring.

Rnd 1: Ch 1, 20 sc in ring, sl st between ch 1 and first sc. (20 scs)

Rnd 2: (Ch 4, dc in next st) around, end with sl st in 3rd ch of beg, sl st in first ch-1 sp.

Rnd 3: Ch 3, 2 dc in same sp (3dc in next ch-1 sp) 3 times, *ch 5, sk 1 sp (3dc in next ch-1

sp) 4 times, repeat from * end with ch 2, join to afghan with sc in 5th sp past corner along bottom edge, ch 2, sl st in top of beg ch of border medallion to close. Fasten off. Second Medallion: Work same as first medallion to the first ch 5 corner of 3rd rnd; ch only 2, skip 4 sps along bottom edge of afghan (moving to the right of last joined border medallion) sc in next sp, sk 1 sp of 2nd medallion, continue around 2nd medallion as for previous one, to next ch 5, ch only 2, attach to previous border medallion at corner with sc, ch 2, continue around 2nd medallion, end with ch 5, sl st in top of beg ch. Fasten off. Continue adding new medallions along bottom edge of afghan in same manner to corner. Make an afghan medallion working 3 sides of 3rd rnd, except ch 5 in corners instead of ch 7, work along the last side 3 dc in 2 sps then sc into corner sp of afghan, work 3 dc in next 2 sps, ch 2, sc in corner of previous border medallion, ch 2 sl st in top of ch 3. Fasten off. Continue to make and add border medallions, working afghan medallions for the other 3 corners. Work along bottom edge in open spaces.

Flower insert: Ch 4, sl st in first ch to make a ring.

Rnd 1: Ch 3, work a cluster in ring as follows: holding back last loop of each dc, work 2 dc, yo, pull through all 3 loops on hook, ch 2. Working in second space from corner, attach to border with sc in center of the 4th 2-dc shell from joining of border medallion to border, ch 2, work a cluster, holding back last loop of each dc work 3 dc, in ring, yo, pull through all 4 loops on hook, ch 2, sk 1 shell of border, sc in center of next shell, ch 2, work cluster in ring, ch 2, sc between the first and second dc groups of border medallion to left, ch 2, work a cluster in ring, ch 2, sk 2 dc sections, sc between next sections, ch 2, work a cluster in ring, ch 2, sc between next 2 dc sections of next border medallion to right, ch 2, work a cluster in ring, ch 2 sk 2 dc sections, sc between next sections, ch 2, sl st in top of beg ch. Fasten off. (6 petals) Work flower inserts in each space around afghan except one on each side of corners. These inserts are worked in same way except they have 5 petals and are attached to corner of border medallion between dc sections in only one place.

Summer White Sachet

Nothing stirs memories better than the sense of smell. Now you can fill your home with the sweet scent of fresh cut flowers in these decorative sachets. The ornament, inspired by blooming flowers, would surely recall a lovely spring day when hung on a holiday tree.

MATERIALS:
Cebelia #20 White - 1 ball (405 yards per ball)
Size 8 steel hook

GAUGE:
 3 rows dc = 1″
 12 dc = 1″

Ch 6, join with sl st in first ch to form a circle.

Rnd 1: Ch 3, work 13 dc in circle, join with sl st in top of beg ch (14 sts).

Rnds 2 & 3: Ch 3, dc in sl st, 2 dc in each dc around, end and join with sl st in top of beg ch (28 sts after rnd 2 and 56 sts after rnd 3).

Rnd 4: Ch 3, dc in each dc around, join with sl st in top of beg ch (56 sts).

Rnd 5: Ch 3, (2 dc in next dc, 1 dc in next dc) around, end with sl st in top of beg ch (84 sts).

Rnd 6: Ch 4, work a cluster as follows: [* (wrap thread over hook twice, insert hook in sl st, thread over and draw through 2 loops) twice, hold back last loop, repeat from * once, thread over and draw through all 3 loops, ch 1. Sk 1 dc, repeat between * once, except insert hook in next dc instead of the sl st, repeat from * twice, except insert hook in same st, thread over and draw through all 4 loops, ch 1], repeat around, end with sl st in top of beg ch (42 clusters).

Rnd 7: Ch 4, (counts as dc, ch 1), * dc in the top ch-1 sp of cluster, ch 1, repeat from * around, end with sl st in 3rd ch of beg ch (42 dc). Sl st in ch-1 sp.

Rnd 8: Ch 4, work a cluster as in rnd 6 in each ch-1 sp, ch 1 between each cluster.

Rnd 9: Repeat rnd 7.

Rnd 10: Repeat rnd 8.

Rnd 11: Repeat rnd 7.

Rnd 12: Ch 4, trc in the sl st (2 trc in next dc, 2 trc in next ch 1 sp) around, end with sl st in top of beg ch.

Rnd 13: Ch 5, (trc in next trc, ch 1) around, join with sl st in top of beg ch.

Rnd 14: Sl st in ch-1 sp, (ch 7, sl st in next ch 1) around, join with sl st in beg ch-1 sp.

Rnd 15: Sl st in first loop, * (ch 3, sc in same loop) twice, ch 3, sc in next loop. Repeat from * around, end with sl st in beg st. Fasten off.

Rose Center Sachet

MATERIALS:
Cebelia #30 Ivory - 1 ball (563
  yards per ball)
Size 8 steel hook

GAUGE:

4 rows dc = 1″
20 dc = 1″

Work same rose as in " **A
Bridal Basket** " for 11 rnds
except do not fasten off
thread. Sl st to center of next
loop between picots.

Rnd 12: Ch 1, sc in same
place, (ch 8, sc in center of
next loop) around, end with sl
st in first sc.

Rnd 13: Ch 1, sc in sc, ch 2, *
16 dc in next sp, ch 2, sc in
next sc, ch 8, sc in next sc,
repeat from * 10 times, end
with ch 4, trc in beg sc.

Rnd 14: Sc in same loop, * ch
8, sc in the 4th dc of group, ch
8, sk 8 dc, sc in next dc, ch 8,
sc in next loop, repeat from *,
do not complete round, end
with ch 4, trc in loop just

before the beg loop (30 loops).
Turn.

Row 15: (Rows 15 and 16 are
not full rnds). Sc in same loop,
(ch 8, sc in next loop) across
until 28 loops are completed,
ch 4, trc in next loop (29
loops). Turn.

Row 16: Sc in same loop, ch 8,
sc in next loop, * ch 4, 9 dc in
next loop, ch 4 sc in next loop,
ch 8, sc in next loop, repeat
from * across (9 dc sections
and 10 ch-8 loops). Do not
turn, continue working around.

Rnd 17: * Sc in next sp, ch 2, 5
dc, ch 2, sc in same sp, repeat
from * once, 5 sc in each of
next 2 sps, repeat between *
twice [(sc, ch 2, 9 dc, ch 2, sc)
in next sp, (sc, ch 2, 4 dc) in
next sp, dc over next 9 dc, (4
dc, ch 2, sc) in next sp] repeat
8 times, end with sc, ch 2, 9
dc, ch 2, sc in last sp, sl st in
beg sc. Fasten off.

Finishing: Run ribbon through
loops beginning at point of
rnd 12.

Victorian Ornament

SIZE: 8″ diameter

MATERIALS:
Cebelia #30 Ivory - 1 ball (563
   yards per ball)
Size 10 steel hook
3″ clear glass ornament - 1

GUAGE: 12 dc = 1″
          4 rows dc = 1″

Rnd 1: Ch 6, dc in 6th ch from
hook, (ch 2, dc in same st) 6
times, ch 2, sl st in 3rd ch of
starting ch.

Rnd 2: (Sc, ch 2, 3 dc, ch 2, sc)
in each ch 2 sp around.

Rnd 3: Sl st to center of next
petal, * ch 7, sc in 5th st from
hook (picot made), (ch 6, sc in
4th ch) twice, ch 3, sc in center of next petal. Repeat from
* 7 times.

Rnd 4: Sl st to sp between 1st
and 2nd picots, sc, * (ch 7, sc
in 5th ch from hook - picot)
twice, ch 2, sc between next 2
picots of same loop, picot
twice, ch 2, sk across last

picot of loop and first picot of
next loop, sc. Repeat from *
around, end with sl st in beg
sc.

Rnds 5-10: Sl st to center of
loop between 2 picots, sc, *
(picot twice, ch 2, sc in center
of next loop) around, end with
sl st in first sc.

Rnd 11: Sl st to center of next
loop, ch 1, sc, in same place, *
in next sc work (trc, make
picot: ch 4, sc in top of trc) 6
times, sc in center of next loop
between picots. 2 trc in next
sc of row below. Make a flower
as follows: ch 1, sc in top of
trc just made (ch 2, 3 dc, ch 2,
sc) 3 times in same place. 2
trc, in same sc of row below
flower. 2 trc in same sc of row
below, sc in center of next
loop. Repeat from * around,
end with sl st in beg sc. Run
ribbon through loops of one
rnd and pull closed around
sachet. Tie.

Hanging Potpourri Cups

MATERIALS:
Balger Pearl 032 Blending Filament - 2 spools (10 M)
Size 8 steel hook

GAUGE: 3 rows trc = 1″
24 trc = 1″

Ch 6, sl st in first ch to form a circle.

Rnd 1: Ch 4, 23 trc in circle, sl st in top of ch 4 (24).

Rnd 2: Sc in first trc, (ch 7, sk 1 trc, sc in next trc), around, end with ch 4, trc in beg sc (12 loops).

Rnd 3: (Ch 5, sc in center ch of next loop) around, end with sl st in first st of beg ch (12 loops).

Rnd 4: Ch 4, 5 trc in next sp, ch 1, (6 trc in next sp, ch 1) eleven times, end with sl st in top of beg ch 4.

Rnd 5: Sc in ch 1 just made, (ch 7, sc in ch-1 sp) around, end with ch 4, trc in beg sc.

Rnd 6: (Ch 5, sc in top of trc just made) three times, * ch 5, sc in center ch of next loop, (ch 5, sc in same place) three times. Repeat from * around, end with ch 3, dc in beg st.

Rnd 7: Sc in top of dc just made, * ch 6, trc in center loops, ch 3, trc in same loop, ch 6, sc in center ch of next loop of row below. Repeat from * around, end with dtrc in beg sc. Turn.

Rnd 8: Sl st in next ch-3 sp, sc in same sp, turn, ch 3, sc in same sp, * ch 4, sc in next ch-3 sp, (ch 3, sc in same sp) three times, 3 picot loops made, repeat from * around, end with sc, ch 3, sc in beg loop, ch 2, dc in beg sc.

Rnd 9: Sc in center loop just created, (ch 9, sc in center loop of 3 picot loops) around, end with ch 9, sl st in beg sc.

Rnd 10: 9 Sc in each loop around, end with sl st in beg sc.

Handle: Ch 18, 1 sc at side of nut cup, in center of 3 picot loop of rnd 6. Turn, work 24 sc in loop just made. Fasten off. Sk 6 loops.

2nd Handle: Attach thread to opposite side of nut cup in top of center loop of 3 picot loops, work same as other handle. Fasten off.

A Bridal Basket

Societies the world around place the highest value upon the ceremony of marriage. For this wedding, we found a rich satin basket and added our crocheted trim for an extra touch. The aromatic sachet is a reminder of a perfect garden wedding. We are sure the bride will treasure these beautiful keepsakes as her thoughts linger back to that glorious day.

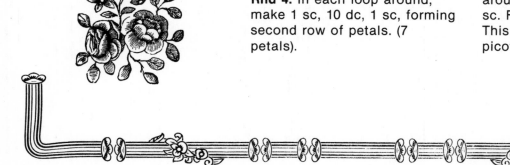

MATERIALS:
Cebelia #30 Ivory - 6 balls (563 yards per ball)
Cebelia #30 White - 6 balls (563 yards per ball)
Size 8 steel hook
500 small Off-White pearl beads 123T
Small amount Wondersheen or #5 Perle cotton

GAUGE:
4 rows dc = 1″
20 dc = 1″
Make 8 roses with Ivory thread.

Rose: Ch 7 join with sl st to form a circle.

Rnd 1: Ch 6, (dc in circle, ch 3) 6 times, join with sl st to 3rd ch of ch-6 (7 sps).

Rnd 2: In each sp around, make 1 sc, 8 dc, 1 sc (7 petals). Join with sl st in 1st sc.

Rnd 3: (Ch 5, working behind rnd 2 petals, sc in next dc of first rnd) around, end with ch 5, sc in same place as sl st on first rnd.

Rnd 4: In each loop around, make 1 sc, 10 dc, 1 sc, forming second row of petals. (7 petals).

Rnd 5: (Ch 6, working behind rnd 4 petals sc in sc between next 2 petals on 3rd rnd) around, end with sc between last and first petals.

Rnd 6: In each loop around, make 1 sc, 12 dc, 1 sc. (Making 7 petals) sl st in 1st sc of rnd.

Rnd 7: (Ch 7, sc in sc between next 2 petals on 5th rnd) around.

Rnd 8: In each loop around, make 1 sc, 14 dc, 1 sc, end with sl st in first sc. Sl st in 1st sc of rnd. Fasten off.

Rnd 9: Join white in 3rd dc of first petal, sc in same place, * (ch 6, sl st in 4th ch from hook - picot made, ch 6, sl st in 4th ch from hook - picot made, ch 2, sk 3 dc, sc in next dc) two times. (Ch 2, picot) two times, ch 2, sc in 3rd dc of next petal, repeat from * around, end with sl st in first sc.

Rnds 10-11: Sl st to center of next loop, sc in same loop, * (ch 2, picot) two times, ch 2, sc in next loop. Repeat from * around, end with sl st in first sc. Fasten off after rnd 11. This completes 3 rnds of white picot loops.

Thistle: Make 8 ivory thistles.

Rnd 1: Wind thread around small finger 20 times, slip off carefully. Make 21 sc in circle of thread. Join with sl st in first sc.

Rnd 2: Ch 6, * trc in next sc, ch 2, repeat from * around, join last ch 2 with sl st in 4th ch of ch 6 (21 sps).

Rnd 3: Carry 2 strands Wondersheen or Perle Cotton around next rnd working over them. Make 4 sc in each sp around, join sl st.

Rnd 4: Sc in same place as sl st, * ch 4, sc in front loop only of next sc. Repeat from * around, end with sl st in first sc. Fasten off.

Rnd 5: Attach white thread in sl st just finished. Sc in same place as sl st * (ch 2, picot) two times, ch 2, sk 3 sc, sc in back loop of next sc. Repeat from * around, join with sl st on first sc.

Rnd 6: Sl st to center of next loop. Repeat rnd 5.
After rose and thistle sections have been worked, set the completed rose together with thistle as follows:

Attaching Rnd: Sl st to center of next loop, sc in same loop, ch 2, picot, ch 1, sl st in any loop on last round of rose, ch 1, picot, ch 2, sc in next loop on thistle, complete as for last round of rose, joining 2nd and 3rd loops to corresponding loops of rose as first loop was joined. Work 7 more picot loops on thistle then join next 3 loops to another rose section. Complete picot loops to end of round (8 more loops). Fasten off.
Set 8 roses and 8 thistles together alternating around to make a circle.

Note: 8 free loops on outer edge; 7 free loops on inner edge of each section.
Work around inner edge as follows:

Rnd 1: Attach white thread to 2nd free loop on any flower, sc in same loop, * (ch 2, picot) two times, ch 2, sc in next loop, repeat from * 4 more times, ch 2, picot, ch 2, sc in next free loop or next flower, turn, (ch 2, picot) two times, ch 2, sc in last loop on previous flower, turn (ch 2, picot) twice, ch 2, sc in last loop made, ch

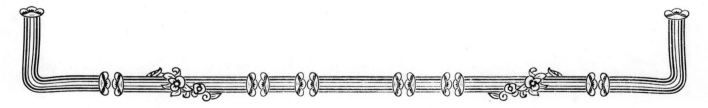

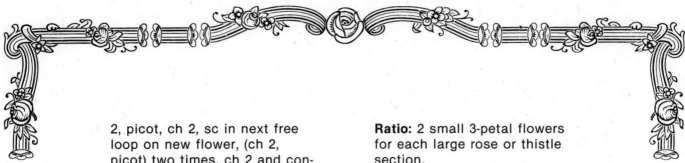

2, picot, ch 2, sc in next free loop on new flower, (ch 2, picot) two times, ch 2 and continue in the same manner around. Join and fasten off. Set aside.

Links: (white) Ch 3, dc in first ch, * ch 3, dc between ch and dc (2 links made). Repeat from * until desired number of links are made. Make 136 links, join with sl st to first link to form a circle. Sc in center of same link, ch 3, dc in same link, ch 1, * 2 dc in next link, ch 1, repeat from * around, end with sl st in top of ch 3. Fasten off. This forms a heading row through which ribbon may be inserted later.

Make 32 Flowers - 3-petal flowers:

Attach ivory thread in center of any ch 1 sp of heading.

Rnd 1: Sc in same st as joining, * (ch 2, picot) two times, ch 8, sl st in 6th ch from hook (this ch-6 loop is center of flower), turn, (ch 5, sc in center loop) 3 times, turn, in each of last three ch-5 loops made (sc, 7 dc, sc), sc in ch-6 loop at center of flower, ch 2, picot, ch 1, sc between first and second picots, ch 2, picot, ch 2, sk 1 sp, sc in next sp, (ch 2, picot) two times, ch 2, sk 4 sc, sc in next sc. Repeat from * around (32 flowers). Fasten off.

Ratio: 2 small 3-petal flowers for each large rose or thistle section.

Rnd 2: Attach white thread to 5th dc of first petal, (counting from stem), (ch 2, picot) 3 times, ch 2, sc in center of 2nd petal, * (ch 2, picot) 3 times, ch 2, sc in 3rd dc on 3rd petal, ch 2, trc in center of next loop between picots, ch 2, sc in 5th dc on first petal of next flower, ch 2, picot, ch 1, turn, sc between first and second picots of last picot, turn, (ch 2, picot) twice, ch 2, sc in center of 2nd petal. Repeat from * around, to join work, ch 2, 2 picots, ch 2, sc between first and second picot of first flower at beg of rnd, ch 2, picot, ch 2 trc in last picot ch of previous rnd between picots, ch 2, sc in beg sc. Join rose and thistle section to center heading section as follows: sl st to center of first loop directly above trc, ch 2, picot, ch 2, sc in center loop between rose and thistle joining. * (Ch 2, picot, ch 2, sc in next loop of heading section, ch 2, picot, ch 2, sc in next loop of rose section). Repeat 3 more times, ch 2, picot, ch 2, sc in sc between 3-petal flowers of previous row, ch 2, picot, ch 2, sc in next rose section. Repeat from * around. Fasten off.

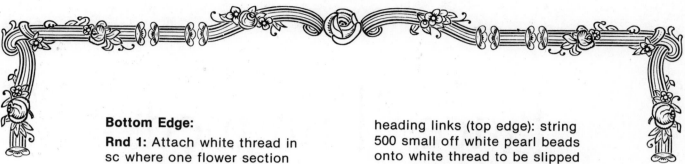

Bottom Edge:

Rnd 1: Attach white thread in sc where one flower section joins another. [ch 2, picot, ch 2, sc in center of next loop, * (ch 2, picot) two times, ch 2, sc in next loop, repeat from * 6 times more. Ch 2, picot, ch 2, sc in sc where next two flower sections join], repeat around, end with sl st in first sc, end, sl st in beg sc.

Rnd 2: Sl st backward to last picot, sc through this picot and next picot together, * (ch 9, sc in next loop) 7 times, sc through next 2 picots together, repeat from * around, end with sl st in beg sc. Fasten off.

Rnd 3: Join ivory thread in last loop just made, ch 1, sc in same loop, * (ch 6, sl st in 4th ch from hook - picot), two times, ch 2, sc in next loop, repeat from * once. [ch 9, sc in next loop, turn. Ch 6, sc in loop just made, ch 9, sc in same loop, ch 6, sc in next sc, turn. Work 6 sc in first loop, work 6 dc, make a picot of ch 4, sl st in top of dc just made, 6 dc, in next (center) loop, work 6 sc in next loop, sc in sc. (Ch 6, sl st in 4th ch for picot) two times, ch 2, sc in next loop] 3 times. Repeat from * to this point around entire outer edge of ring of motifs, end with sl st in beg sc. Working on other side of

heading links (top edge): string 500 small off white pearl beads onto white thread to be slipped into place and crocheted into work as required. (Beads slip to back of work so you must work on wrong side of work).

Rnd 1: Attach thread into center of any link, ch 3, slip a bead (b) up and ch 1, * (dc in same link, ch 1, dc in same link, b, ch 1) 3 times, sk 1 link, dc, b, ch 1 in next link, repeat from * around, end with sl st in top of beg ch-3.
Slide bead down thread. No beads are used in next rnd.

Rnd 2: Ch 1, * sc in the ch-1 sp, between shells, ch 2, (dc in next ch-1 sp, ch 2) 6 times, repeat from * around, end with sl st in beg sc. Use beads for next rnd.

Rnd 3: * b, sc in next sp, (ch 6, picot in 4th ch, ch 3, sk 1 sp, b, sc in next sp) 3 times, ch 3, repeat from * around, end with sl st in beg sc. Fasten off. Join ivory thread and working on right side attach in ch-3 sp just made.

Rnd 4: * (Ch 6, picot in 4th ch) two times, ch 3, sc in next loop just past the picot, (ch 6, picot) two times, ch 3, sk 1 picot loop, sc just before the picot in next loop, (ch 6, picot) two times, ch 3, sc in next loop, repeat from * around, end with sl st in beg ch.

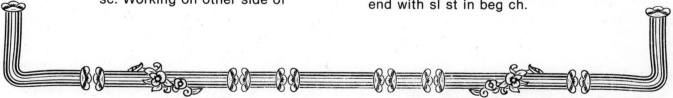

Lace Trimmed Sachet

MATERIALS:
Cordonnet #50 Natural - 1 ball
  (286 yards per ball)
Size 12 steel hook

GAUGE:
7 rows dc = 1″
15 dc = 1″

Row 1: Ch 12, dc in 6th ch from hook, ch 2, dc in same place, ch 2, sk next 2 chs, sc in next st, ch 2, sk next 2 chs, (dc ch 2, dc) in next st, ch 3, turn.

Row 2: (Dc, ch 2, dc) in 1st sp, ch 3, sk 2 sps, 5 dc in next sp, ch 5, turn.

Row 3: (Dc, ch 2, dc) in 3rd dc, ch 2, sc in ch-4 loop, ch 2, (dc, ch 2, dc) in next ch-2 sp, ch 3, turn. Repeat rows 2 and 3 to desired length. Work row 2 once more.

Row 1: Turn and work down the side in the ch-5 sp as follows: * ch 2, [(dc, ch 1) 6 times, dc], in first ch-5 sp, ch 2, sc in next ch-5 sp. Repeat from * to end. Turn.

Row 2: * ch 3, dc in first ch-1 sp, (ch 5, dc in next ch-1 sp) 5 times, ch 3, sc in sc. Repeat from * to end.

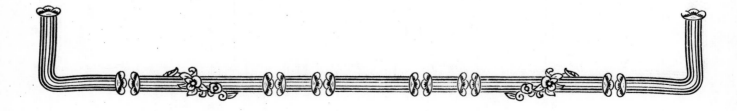

Linen Sachet

MATERIALS:

12" of completed crocheted
edging

One 12" × 11" white handker-
chief linen fabric; matching
thread

12" length of ¼" beige cotton
lace

12" length of ⅛" cream cotton
lace

Twelve pearl buttons

12" of white bias tape

2¾ yards of ⅛"–wide white
satin ribbon

Potpourri

DIRECTIONS:

All seams are ¼".

1. By hand, attach the beige
lace 1" below one 12" edge of
the linen fabric. Attach the
cream lace 1 ½" below the 12"
edge.

2. By machine, make two button holes (Diagram 1).

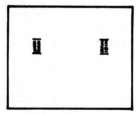

3. Stitch 11" edges with right
sides together. Refold the fabric to measure 5¾" × 11".
(Diagram 2). Stitch across the
bottom edge.

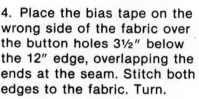

4. Place the bias tape on the
wrong side of the fabric over
the button holes 3½" below
the 12" edge, overlapping the
ends at the seam. Stitch both
edges to the fabric. Turn.

5. Stitch a narrow hem in the
top edge folded toward the
right side of the bag. By hand,
attach the crocheted edging
over the hem. Attach the buttons 1" apart on the cream
lace.

6. Cut the white ribbon into
four 27" lengths. Thread two,
handling them as a single unit,
into buttonhole and work
through the casing and exit
through the same buttonhole.
Repeat with the remaining ribbon in and out of the second
buttonhole.

7. Fill the bag with potpourri.
Draw up the ribbons and tie
into bows.

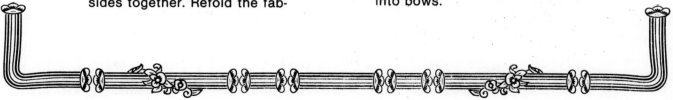

Cream Satin Stocking

The holidays are the time to bring out our best. Festooned with delicate crocheted edgings, these stockings and ornaments add spirit to any holiday gathering.

SIZE: 9″ × 2½″

MATERIALS:
Balger Blending Filament cable gold 002P - 1 spool (10 M)
Cebelia #20 Natural - 1 ball (405 yards per ball)
Size 7 steel hook

GAUGE:
4 rows dc = 2½″
25 dc = 2½″

Ch links with Cebelia: Ch 4, dc in 3rd ch from hook, * ch 3, dc in sp between ch 3 and dc. (2 links made) Repeat from * until desired number of links are made.

Row 1: Make 28 ch-3 links, sl st into first link on ch-3 side, (ch 3, dc, ch 1, 2 dc) in same link, [(ch 1, 2 dc) in next link], repeat to last link, end with ch 1, (2 dc, ch 1, 2 dc) in last link. Turn.

Row 2: Ch 5, (trc, ch 1, trc) in next ch-1 sp, ch 3, [sk 1 sp, (trc, ch 1, trc) in next sp, ch 3] 13 times, end with trc, ch 1, trc in next sp, trc in last dc of row below. Turn.

Row 3: Sc in next ch-1 sp, * ch 3, sc in same sp, ch 5, sc in next ch-1 sp, (4 trc, ch 3, sl st to make picot in top of last trc just made, 4 trc) in next ch-3 sp, sc in next ch-1 sp, ch 5, sc in next ch-1 sp, repeat from * across row, end with ch 3, sc in same sp. Turn.

Row 4: Ch 6, (trc, ch 1, trc) in first ch-5 link, * ch 5, sc in picot, [ch 5, (trc, ch 1, trc) in next ch-5 sp] twice, repeat from * end with ch 5, trc, ch 1, trc in next ch-5 sp, ch 1, trc in

top of last trc of row 2, just beyond last picot of row 3 (last st). Turn.

Row 5: Ch 4, trc in next ch-1 sp, ch 3, sc in next ch-1 sp, * ch 3, sc in next ch-5 sp, ch 3, sc in next sc (above picot) ch 3, sc in next ch-5 sp, ch 3, sc in next ch-1 sp, ch 5, sc in ch-5 sp, ch 5, sc in next ch-1 sp, repeat from * across, end with ch 3, sc in next ch-5 sp, ch 3, sc in next sc, ch 3, sc in next ch-5 sp, ch 3, sc in next ch-1 sp, ch 3, 2 trc in last sp. Turn.

Row 6: Ch 3, sc in first ch-3 sp, * (ch 3, sc in next ch-3 sp) 4 times, ch 3, 2 dc in ch-5 sp, ch 1, 2 dc in next ch-5 sp, repeat from *, end with dc in last ch-3 sp, dc in top of last st. Turn.

Row 7: Ch 3, (dc, ch 1, dc) in sp between last 2 dc of row below, (ch 3, sc in next sp) 3 times, * ch 5, 2 dc between next 2 dc, 2 dc in ch-1 sp, 2 dc between next 2 dc, ch 5, (sc in next sp, ch 3) twice, sc in next sp, repeat from *, end with ch 5, 3 dc in last ch-3 sp. Turn.

Row 8: Ch 3, dc between next 2 sts, ch 1, 2 dc between next 2 sts, * ch 5, sc in next ch sp, ch 3, sc in next ch sp, ch 5, work a shell of (2 dc, ch 1, 2

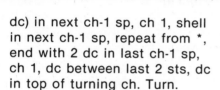

dc) in next ch-1 sp, ch 1, shell in next ch-1 sp, repeat from *, end with 2 dc in last ch-1 sp, ch 1, dc between last 2 sts, dc in top of turning ch. Turn.

Row 9: Ch 3, dc between next 2 sts, ch 1, shell in next ch-1 sp, * ch 5, sc in ch-3 loop, ch 5, shell in ch-1 sp of next shell, ch 1, shell in next ch-1 sp, ch 1, shell in ch-1 sp of next shell, repeat from *, end with shell in last ch-1 sp, ch 1, dc between last 2 sts, dc in top of turning ch. Turn. Fasten off.

Row 10: (with gold thread) Ch 1, sc in same place (ch 3, sc in next ch sp) 3 times, * ch 3, sc over sc, (ch 3, sc in next ch sp) 7 times, repeat from * across, end with (ch 3, sc in next ch sp) 3 times, ch 3, sc in top of turning ch.

TRIM (heel and toe)

SIZE: 10″ × 1½″ wide

MATERIALS:
Cebelia #30 Ivory - 1 ball (563 yards per ball)
DMC Fil or clair Gold - 1 spool (40 M per spool)
Size 7 steel hook

Make one for toe and one for heel. With Ivory Cebelia, make 27 ch 3 links, turn.

Links: Ch 3, dc in first ch, * ch 3, dc between ch 3 and dc (2 links made) repeat from * until 27 links are made.

Row 1: Working down the ch-3 side of links, 5 sc in first link, (ch 5, sk 1 link, 5 sc in next link) across, turn.

Row 2: Ch 1, (sc in next 5 sc, ch 5, sc in next loop, ch 5) across, end with sc in last 5 sts, turn.

Row 3: Ch 1, sk 1 sc, * sc in next 3 sc, (ch 5, sc in next loop) twice, ch 5, sk 1 sc, repeat from * across, end with sc in next 4 sc, turn.

Row 4: Ch 1, * sc in center sc, (ch 5, sc in next loop) 3 times, ch 5, repeat from * across, end with sc in center sc, sc in last st, turn. Fasten off.

Row 5: (Gold thread) (ch 5, sc in each loop) across, turn.

Row 6: * (Ch 5, sc in next loop) 3 times, ch 5, work a cluster of 3 dc holding back last loop of each, thread over, pull through all 4 loops on hook, repeat from * across, end with (ch 5, sc in next loop) 4 times. Fasten off.

CREAM STOCKING

MATERIALS:

9½" of crochet border for stocking top

12" of crochet ruffle for toe and 10" of crochet ruffle for heel

½ yard of cream satin; matching thread

½ yard of cream polyester lining

½ yard of polyester fleece

2¼" yards of ½"-wide white/gold ribbon

¼ yard of ⅞"-wide black with gold dots ribbon

¼ yard of 1½"-wide black/gold grosgrain ribbon

1 yard of ⅝"-wide white/gold grosgrain ribbon

½ yard of 1½"-wide white/gold grosgrain ribbon

⅛ yard of ⅝"-wide cream satin ribbon

Five ½"-wide to ¾"-wide antique brass buttons

Dressmaker's Pen

DIRECTIONS:

All seams are ¼".

1. Enlarge stocking pattern. Cut two stocking pieces from cream satin, two stocking pieces from lining fabric and one stocking piece from fleece.

2. Mark the heel and toe lines on the stocking front; see pattern. Mark the placement for ribbons, planning which will have ends tucked under other strips. Set aside the remainders. Sew the buttons to the stocking front.

3. By hand, sew the ribbons to the stocking front. Sew the crochet pieces to the heel and toe.

4. Pin the fleece to the wrong side of the stocking front piece. Stitch the right sides of satin stocking pieces together, securing the fleece in the seam. Trim the fleece from the seam allowance. Clip the curved edges. Turn.

5. Stitch the two lining pieces together, leaving a large opening in the side seam above the heel.

6. Fold a 6" piece of 1½" wide white/gold grosgrain ribbon to measure 3". Pin the raw ends of the ribbon over the right side seam for loop. Slide the lining over the stocking. Match the side seams of the stocking and lining with the right sides together. Stitch around the top edge of the stocking. Turn through the opening in the lining.

7. By hand, sew crochet for stocking top to the stocking front, attaching the edges to the side seam.

8. Fold the remaining ½" wide white/gold ribbon into two 6" wide loops with ends loose. Tie the remaining ⅝" wide white/gold grosgrain around the center of the loops to make a bow. Tack the bow to the upper right corner. Trim the ends.

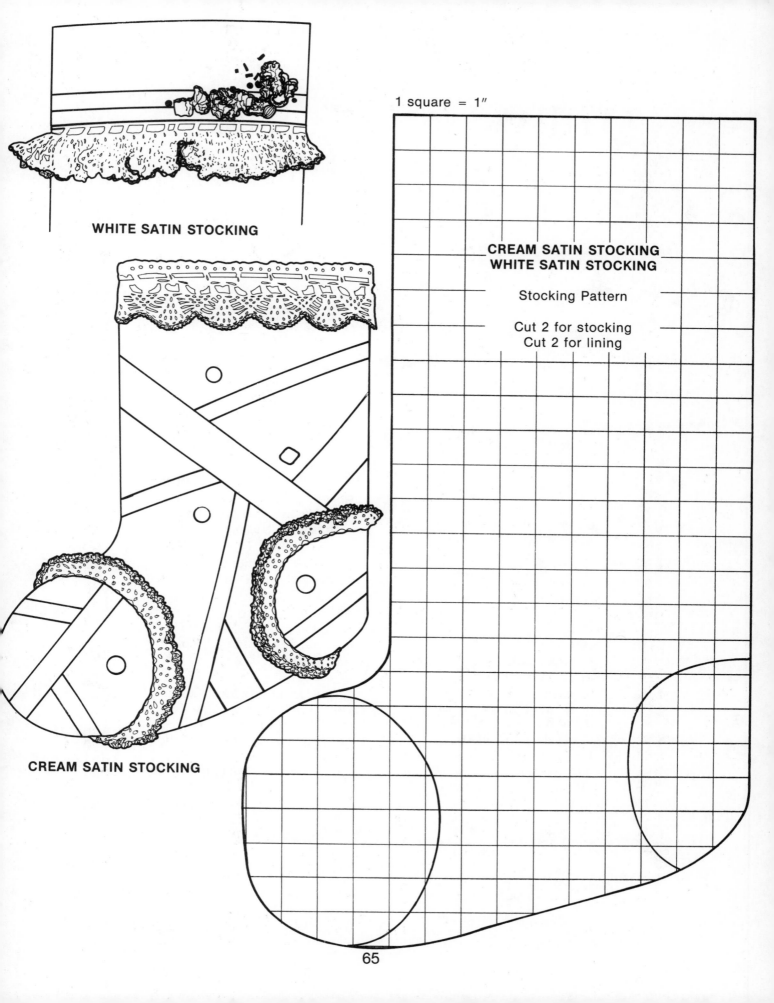

WHITE SATIN STOCKING

1 square = 1"

CREAM SATIN STOCKING
WHITE SATIN STOCKING

Stocking Pattern

Cut 2 for stocking
Cut 2 for lining

CREAM SATIN STOCKING

White Stocking Ruffle

SIZE: 18″ × 2″

MATERIALS:
Cebelia #30 White - 1 ball (563
    yards per ball)
Size 10 steel hook
Balger Gold 002P blending fila-
    ment - 2 spools
(100 M)

GAUGE: 12 dc = 1″
        4 rows dc = 1″

Ch links with Cebelia: Ch 4, dc
in 3rd ch from hook, * ch 3, dc
in sp between ch 3 and dc. (2
links made) Repeat from * until
desired number of links are
made. Make 60 links.

Row 1: Sl st in center of first
link, ch 4, trc in same link, *
ch 2, 2 trc in next link, repeat
from * to end (60 sps). Turn.

Row 2: * Ch 7, sc in next sp,
(ch 7, sc in same sp) twice,
repeat from * to end. Ch 1,
turn.

Rows 3-6: Sc in loop just
made, (ch 7, sc in next loop) to
end. Ch 1, turn.

Row 7: Sc in loop just made, *
ch 3, (3 dc, 3 trc, 3 dc) in next
loop, ch 3, sc in next loop,
repeat from * to end. Fasten
off.

Row 8: (gold thread) Attach
with sc in same sc, * ch 4, sc
in 2nd dc of group, ch 4, sc in
center trc of same group, ch 4,
sc in next to last dc of same
group, ch 4, sc in sc, repeat
from * to end. Fasten off.

The **White Stocking Ruffle** crochet is also used around the lid on p. 43.

66

WHITE SATIN STOCKING

MATERIALS:

18" of crochet ruffle
One crocheted ornament; see
Delicate Heart Ornament
¾ yard of white satin; matching thread
½ yard of polyester fleece
¾ yard of white polyester lining fabric
1½ yards of ¼"–wide gold ribbon
⅝ yard of ½"–wide white/gold ribbon
⅝ yard of ¼"–wide white ribbon
4½ yards of variegated chiffon ribbon
4 yards of green/gold twisted cord
6" of 2¼"–wide white satin ribbon
One ¾"–wide decorative metal button
One ⅜"–wide gold bead
Two ⅛"–wide brass faceted beads
One ⅛"–wide copper faceted beads
One ⅛"–wide blue faceted beads
Four copper bugle beads
Two black beads

DIRECTIONS:

All seams are ¼".

1. Enlarge stocking pattern. Cut two stocking pieces and one 9" × 18½" piece for cuff from white satin. Cut two stocking pieces from lining fabric. Cut one stocking piece from fleece.

2. Pin fleece to wrong side of stocking front piece. Stitch right sides of satin stocking piece together, securing fleece in seam. Trim fleece from seam allowance. Clip curved edges. Turn.

3. Stitch two lining pieces together, leaving a large opening in the side seam above heel.

4. Fold cuff piece with right sides together, to measure 9" × 9¼". Stitch side seam. Refold cuff piece to measure 18" × 4½" right side out. By hand, sew ½"–wide gold/white ribbon 1" above and parallel to fold of cuff. Cut one 45" length of chiffon ribbon. Pull a thread near the edge opposite the gold. Gather tightly. Tack to stocking cuff (see diagram). Add beads and button.

5. Slide cuff over stocking and pin matching raw edges and side seam. Fold 6" piece of 2¼"–wide ribbon to measure 3". Pin raw ends of ribbon over right side seam for loop. Slide lining over stocking. Match side seams of stocking and lining with right sides together. Stitch around top edge of stocking. Turn through opening in lining.

6. Sew crochet ruffle to folded edge of cuff. Cut 19" length of varigated chiffon ribbon. Thread through beading. Secure.

7. Add ribbon trim. Tack to upper right corner of stocking.

Heart Ornament

MATERIALS:
Balger Pearl 032-#8 Braid - 3
  spools (10M)
Thread (Kreinik)
Size 8 steel hook
GAUGE:
11 dc = 1″
4 rows dc = 1″

NOTE: Rnds 1-6 are worked in rounds with right side facing. Do not turn.

Rnd 1: Ch 2, hdc in first ch made to form a loop. In center of loop, work sc, hdc, 3 dc, hdc, 3 sc, make a picot as follows: ch 3, sl st in top of last sc, this forms the point of the heart, 3 sc, hdc, 3 dc, hdc, sl st in beg sc.

Rnd 2: Ch 1, sc in next st, hdc in next st, 3 hdc in next st, 2 hdc in next st, hdc in next 4 sts, 3 sc in the picot, hdc in next 4 sts, 2 hdc in next st, 3 hdc in next st, hdc in next st, sc in next st, sl st in beg ch 1.

Rnd 3: Ch 3, dc in next 2 sts, 2 dc in each of next 3 sts, dc in next 6 sts, 2 dc in next st, dc in next st (center point of heart), 2 dc in next st, dc in next 6 sts, 2 dc in each of next 3 sts, dc in next 2 sts, ch 3, sl st in first ch of beg ch 3. (Center top).

Rnd 4: Ch 1, 2 Sc in ch-3 sp, 2 sc in each dc to point of heart, 3 sc in point st, 2 sc in each dc to ch 3, 3 sc in ch-3 sp, sl st in first ch at beg (71 sc).

Rnd 5: Ch 3, sc in 3rd sc, (ch 3, sk 1 sc, sc in next sc) around, end with ch 3, sk last 3 sts, sl st in beg ch of ch 3. (34 loops).

Rnd 6: * Ch 7, sk 1 loop, (working behind rnd 5 loops) sc in the next skipped sc of rnd 4, repeat from *, end with sl st in beg ch of ch 7. (17 loops).

Rnd 7: Sl st to center of first loop, (ch 7, sc in next loop) around, end with ch 3, trc in center ch of last loop of previous rnd (16 loops), turn.

Row 8: * (Ch 6, sc in 4th ch from hook to make a picot) twice, ch 2, sc in next loop. Repeat from * to last loop, end with sc in center ch of last loop of previous rnd, turn.

Row 9: * Ch 9, sc in center of next loop between picots, ch 8, sl st in sc just made, repeat from *, end with ch 9, sc in center of sc (beyond last picot) of rnd 7 on same side. Ch 1, turn.

Row 10: * 10 Sc in next loop, 2 sc in small loop, (picot of ch 3, sc in last sc just made, sc) 3 times, 1 more sc in same loop. Repeat from *, end with sl st in sc at end of row. Sl st to top center of heart. Ch 60, sl st in the first chain to form the hanging loop.

Finishing: Work another heart by working rnds 1 through 5. Leave 15″ of thread, cut and fasten off. Put small heart in place over other heart section, wrong sides together. Stitch through sc's in 4th rnd. Leave half open, insert sachet scent through opening. Finish stitching closed. Using same color thread, sew beads at center point of all loops in rows 6,7 and 8. Sew 2 tear-drop beads on bottom two loops of heart on row 7. Sew one tear drop bead on center bottom loop of last row.

Luminous Ornament

MATERIALS:
Balger Pearl 032 blending filament - 3 spools (100 M)
Size 8 steel hook
3″ clear glass ornament

Ch 4, join with sl st to form a
circle.

Rnd 1: Ch 3, 15 dc in circle.
Join with sl st in top of ch 3.

Rnd 2: Sc in same place as
joining, (ch 3, sc in next dc)
around, end with ch 1, hdc in
first sc.

Rnd 3: Ch 4, trc in loop just
made, (ch 3, 2 trc in next loop)
around, end with ch 3, sl st in
top of ch 4.

Rnd 4: Sc between ch and trc,
[5 dc in next sp (shell made),
sc between next 2 trc] around,
end with shell, sl st in first sc.

Rnd 5: Sl st to center of next
shell, sc in same place, (shell
in next sc, sc in center of next
shell, ch 7, sc in center of next
shell) around, end with ch 7, sl
st in sc.

Rnd 6: Sc in same place, (ch 5,
sc in center of next shell, ch 5,
sc in next sc, ch 5, sc in next
loop, ch 5, sc in next sc, ch 5,
sc in next loop, ch 5, sc in
next sc) around, end ch 2, dc
in first sc.

Rnds 7-13: Sc in loop just
made, (ch 5, sc in next loop)
around, end with ch 2, dc in
first sc.

Rnd 14: Repeat rnd 3, except
ch 5 instead of ch 3.

Rnd 15: Repeat rnd 4, except
work 7 dc shells.

Rnd 16: Work same as rnd 5,
except work 7 dc shells, end
with ch 3, trc in first sc.

Rnd 17: Ch 4, trc in same loop,
(ch 7, 2 trc in next loop)
around, end with ch 4, trc in
top of ch 4.

Rnds 18-23: Sc in same place,
(ch 7, sc in next loop) around,
end ch 4, trc in sc.

Rnd 24: Repeat rnd 14 (beading
row for ribbon).

Rnd 25: Repeat rnd 15 (7 dc
shells).

Rnd 26: Repeat rnd 16 (7 dc
shells).

Rnd 27: Sc in same place, (ch
7, sc in center st of shell, ch 7,
sc in loop) around, end with ch
4, trc in beg sc.

Rnds 28-31: Sc in same place,
(ch 7, sc in next loop) around,
end with ch 4, trc in beg sc.

Rnd 32: Sc in same place, (ch
3, 9 dc shell in next loop, ch 3,
sc in next loop) around, end
with trc in beg sc.

Rnd 33: Sl st in first loop, ch 3,
8 dc in same loop, * ch 3, work
(sc, ch 3, sc) in center of shell
below, ch 3, (9 dc in next loop)
twice. Repeat from * around,
end with (9 dc in next loop)
once. Sl st in top of ch 3 at
beg of rnd.

olden ar ing

MATERIALS:
DMC Gold Filor thread - 1
   spool (43 yards per spool)
Size 10 steel hook
Use 2 strands of thread.

Make 30 links: ch 3, dc in first ch, * ch 3, dc between ch 3 and dc, (2 links made). Repeat from * until 30 links are made. Turn.

Row 1: Sl st in center of first link, ch 3, dc in same link, (ch 2, dc in next link) across, end with 2 dc in last link, turn.

Row 2: (Ch 5, sc in next ch-2 sp) across, end with ch 5, sk 1 dc, sc in top of turning ch, turn.

Row 3: (Ch 6, sc in next loop) across, turn.

Row 4: (Ch 7, sc in next loop) across, turn.

Row 5: (Ch 8, sc in next loop, ch 3, 3 dc in next loop, ch 3, sc in next loop) across, turn.

Row 6: Ch 9, * sc in center dc of dc-group, ch 4, (2 dc, ch 3, 2 dc) in next loop, ch 4, repeat from * across, end with ch 9, sc in last loop, turn.

Fringe: Cut 88 strands, each 5 ½″ long. Place 8 strands together and knot through each end and in the ch-3 sp of each shell. Trim.

Dainty Doily

Small and decorative, doilies remind us of summer afternoons spent as the guest of a favorite aunt. She kept a doily on her dressing table under her mother's silver brush, comb and hand mirror. Another was placed beneath the cut glass vase of freshly cut roses from her garden. For a fresh touch, we have added embroidery and ribbon, just twisted freely and tacked, to our nostalgic doilies.

SIZE: 7 ½″ diameter

MATERIALS:
Cordonnet #30 White - 1 ball
    (216 yards per ball)
Size 12 steel hook
7″ diameter hemstitched linen circle

GAUGE: 5 rows dc = 1″
             24 dc = 1″

PREPARATION: Mark 7″–wide circle. Hemstitch edge of circle. Trim linen close to hemstitching.

EDGE: Base Rnd: Work (sc in 2 holes, 2 sc in third hole) around outside edge of linen circle (multiple of 4 sts).

Rnd 1: * ch 2, sk 3 scs, dc in next sc, working over the dc just made, work 6 sc, sc in same place as beg of ch, repeat from * around to end, sl st in same st as beg ch.

Heart Doily

SIZE: 8 ½" diameter

MATERIALS:
Cordonnet #50 White - 2 balls
(286 yards per ball)
Size 12 steel hook
4 ½" × 4 ½" piece of white
linen

GAUGE:
7 rows dc ^{5} 1"
15 dc = 1"

PREPARATION: Mark 4 ¼"
wide circle. Cut from linen.
Hemstitch around edge of
linen.

EDGE: Base rnd: Work 204 sc
around edge of linen. (Approximately 18 sc per inch)

Rnd 1: Ch 3, dc in each sc
around to end, sl st in top of
ch 3.

Rnd 2: Ch 3, dc in next 11 dcs,
(ch 3, sk 2 dc, dc in next dc,
ch 3, sk 2 dc, dc in next 12
dcs) around to end, ch 3, sk 2
dc, dc in next dc, ch 3, sl st in
top of beg ch 3.

Rnd 3: Sl st in next st, ch 3, dc
over next 10 dc, * ch 3, sk 3
ch, (dc, ch 3, dc) over next dc,
ch 3, sk 3 ch and 1 dc, dc in
next 11 dcs, repeat from *
around to end, ch 3, sk 3 ch,
(dc, ch 3, dc) in next dc, ch 3,
sl st in top of beg ch.

Rnd 4: Sl st in next st, ch 3, dc
over next 9 dcs, * ch 3, dc over
next dc, ch 3, dc over next dc,
ch 3, dc in next 10 dcs, repeat
from * around to end, sl st in
top of beg. ch.

Rnd 5: Sl st in next dc, ch 3,
dc over next 8 dcs, * work a
picot as follows: ch 4, sc in
second ch from hook, ch 1,
(dc, picot, dc) over next dc.
Work picot, sk 3 ch, (dc, picot,
dc) over next dc, repeat from *
around. End with picot. Sl st in
top of beg ch.

Rnd 6: Sl st in next st, ch 3, dc
over next 7 dcs, *(picot, dc in
next dc) 4 times, picot, sk 1 dc,
dc over next 8 dcs, repeat from
* around to end, picot, sl st in
top of beg ch.

Rnd 7: Sl st in next st, ch 3, dc
over next 6 dcs, [* picot, work
(dc, picot, dc) over next dc,
repeat from * 3 times, picot, sk
1 dc, dc in next 7 dcs] repeat
around to end, sl st in top of
beg ch.

Rnd 8: Sl st in next st, ch 3, dc
over next 5 dcs, * (picot, dc
over next dc) 8 times, picot, sk

1 dc, dc in next 6 dcs, repeat
from * around to end, sl st in
top of beg ch.

Rnd 9: Sl st in next st, ch 3, dc
over next 4 dcs, * picot, dc
over next dc, picot (dc, picot,
dc) in next dc, (picot, dc in
next dc) 4 times, picot (dc,
picot, dc) in next dc, picot, dc
in next dc, picot, sk 1 dc, dc in
next 5 dcs, repeat from *
around to end, sl st in top of
beg ch.

Rnd 10: Sl st in next st, ch 3,
dc in next 3 dcs, * (picot, dc in
next dc) 10 times, picot, sk 1
dc, dc in next 4 dcs, repeat
from * around, end with sl st
in top of beg ch.

Rnd 11: Sl st in next st, ch 3,
dc over next 2 dcs, * picot, dc
over next dc, picot, (dc, picot,
dc) in next dc, (picot, dc in
next dc) 6 times, picot, (dc,
picot, dc) in next dc, dc in next
3 dcs, repeat from * around,
end with sl st in top of beg ch.

Rnd 12: Sl st in next st, ch 3,
dc over next dc, * (picot, dc in
next dc) 12 times, picot, sk 1
dc, dc in next 2 dc, repeat
from * around, end with sl st
in beg ch.

Rnd 13: Sl st in next st, ch 3, *
(picot, dc over next dc) 12
times, picot, dc between next 2
dc, repeat from * around, end
with sl st in top of beg ch.
Fasten off.

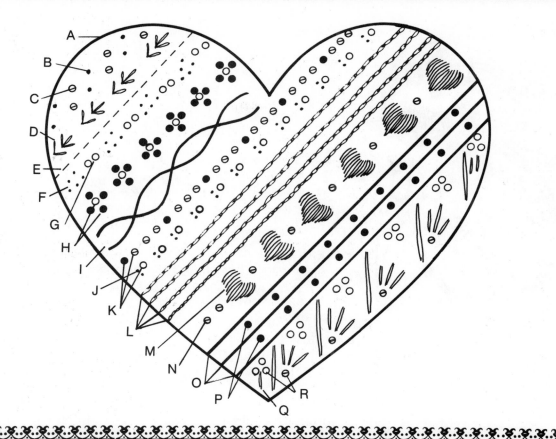

Center the linen over the pattern and, keeping fabric smooth, trace with a water-soluble dressmaker's pen. (It may be necessary to trace the pattern onto a piece of paper, tape it to a window and place the fabric over the paper on the window.)

Complete all embroidery before adding beads. Sew the beads on with one strand of matching embroidery floss, working from lower left to upper right. Secure the beads by returning the thread through the beads, lower right to upper left.

Cut linen into a 7″ circle. Hemstitch the edge.

A. Outline Stitch: 2 strands of DMC 818

B. French Knots: 1 strand, 2 wraps of DMC ecru

C. Beadwork: MPR 123T (cream)

D. Long Stitch: 2 strands of DMC 818

E. Running Stitch: 2 strands of DMC 818

F. French Knots: 1 strand, 2 wraps of DMC ecru

G. Beadwork: MPR 479K (white)

H. Beadwork: MPR 145T (pink) and MPR 479K (white)

I. Outline Stitch: 2 strands of DMC ecru

J. French Knot: 1 strand, 1 wrap of DMC 818

K. Beadwork: MPR 145T (pink), MPR 123T (cream) and MPR 479K (white)

L. Chain Stitch: 2 strands of DMC white

M. Satin Stitch: 2 strands of DMC 818

N. Beadwork: MPR 123T (cream)

O. Outline Stitch: 2 strands of DMC ecru

P. Beadwork: MPR 145T (pink)

Q. Long Stitch: 2 strands of DMC 818

R. Beadwork: MPR 479K (white) and MPR 125T (cream), below each group of 3 Long Stitches

acy Doily

SIZE: 8″ diameter

MATERIALS:
Tatting thread #70 White - 5
    balls (106 yards per ball)
Size 14 steel hook
110 pearl beads

GAUGE:
8 rows dc = 1″
40 dc = 1″

Base Rnd: Ch 8, sl st in first ch to form a circle.

Rnd 1: Ch 1, work 18 sc in circle, end with sl st in first sc.

Rnd 2: Ch 8, sk 2 scs, * dc in next sc, ch 5, sk 2 scs, repeat from * around, end with sl st in 3rd ch (6 loops).

Rnd 3: Ch 1, 5 sc in each sp around, end with sl st in beg ch.

Rnd 4: Ch 8, * sk 2 scs, dc in next sc, ch 5, repeat from * around, end with sl st in 3rd ch of beg ch.

Rnd 5: Ch 1, work (sc, 5 dc, sc) in each loop around, end with sl st in beg ch.

Rnd 6: Sl st to center of petal, ch 1, sc in same place, * ch 8, sc in center of next petal, repeat from * around, end with ch 4, trc in beg sc.

Rnd 7: Ch 3, 5 dc in loop just completed, * ch 8, dc in next loop, ch 8, 5 dc in next loop, repeat from * around, end with ch 4, trc in top of beg ch 3.

Rnd 8: Ch 11, * dc in center dc of 5-dc group, (ch 8, dc in next loop) twice, ch 8, repeat from * around, end with ch 4, trc in 3rd ch of beg ch.

Rnd 9: Ch 3, 4 dc in loop just made, * (ch 8, dc in next loop) twice, ch 8, 5 dc in next loop, repeat from * around, end with ch 4, trc in top of beg ch.

Rnd 10: Ch 11, * dc in center of dc of 5-dc group (ch 8, dc in next loop) 3 times, ch 8, repeat from * around, end with ch 4, trc in 3rd ch of beg ch.

Rnd 11: 4 Sc in loop just made, 8 sc in each loop around, 4 sc in last loop, sl st to join in beg sc.

Rnd 12: Ch 11, dc in center of next loop, ch 8, dc in center of next loop, * ch 8, dc in next dc, (ch 8, dc in center of next loop) twice, repeat from * around, end with ch 4, trc in 3rd ch of beg ch.

Rnd 13: Ch 11, dc in next loop, (ch 8, dc in next loop) twice, * ch 8, 5 dc in next loop, (ch 8, dc in next loop) 5 times, repeat from * around, end with ch 4, trc in 3rd ch of beg ch.

Rnd 14: Ch 11, dc in next loop, (ch 8, dc in next loop) twice, * (ch 8, 5 dc in next loop) twice, (ch 8, dc in next loop) 4 times, repeat from * around, end with ch 4, trc in 3rd ch of beg ch.

Rnd 15: Ch 3, 4 dc in last loop just made, * (ch 8, dc in next loop) 3 times, (ch 8, 5 dc in next loop) 3 times, repeat from * around, end with (ch 8, 5 dc) twice, ch 4, trc in top of beg ch.

Rnd 16: Ch 3, 4 dc in last loop just made, * (ch 8, dc in next loop) 4 times, (ch 8, 5 dc in next loop) twice, repeat from * around, end with 5 dc once, ch

4, trc in top of beg ch.

Rnd 17: Ch 3, 4 dc in last loop just made, * (ch 8, dc in next loop) 6 times, ch 8, dc in center of dc section, ch 8, 5 dc in next loop, repeat from * around, end with dc in center of dc section, ch 4, trc in beg ch.

Rnd 18: Ch 11, dc in next loop, (ch 8, dc in next loop) twice, * ch 8, 5 dc in next loop, (ch 8, dc in next loop) 7 times, repeat from * around, end with ch 4, trc in 3rd ch of beg ch.

Rnd 19: Ch 11, dc in next loop, * (ch 8, dc in next loop) twice, (ch 8, 5 dc in next loop) twice, (ch 8, dc in next loop) 6 times, repeat from * around, end with ch 4, trc in 3rd ch of beg ch.

Rnd 20: Ch 11, dc in next loop, (ch 8, dc in next loop) twice, * (ch 8, 5 dc in next loop) 3 times, (ch 8, dc in next loop) 5 times, repeat from * around, end with ch 4, trc in 3rd ch of beg ch.

Rnd 21: Ch 11, dc in next loop, (ch 8, dc in next loop) 3 times, * (ch 8, 5 dc in next loop) twice, (ch 8, dc in next loop) 6 times, repeat from * around, end with ch 4, trc in 3rd ch of beg ch.

Rnd 22: Ch 11, dc in next loop, (ch 8, dc in next loop) 4 times, * ch 8, dc in center of 5-dc section, ch 8, 5 dc in next loop, ch 8, dc in center of 5-dc section, (ch 8, dc in next loop) 9 times, repeat from * around, end with ch 4, trc in 3rd ch of beg ch.

Rnd 23: Ch 11, 5 dc in next loop, * (ch 8, dc in next loop) 9 times, * ch 8, 5 dc in next loop, repeat from * around, end with ch 4, trc in 3rd ch of beg ch.

Rnd 24: Ch 11, * 5 dc in next loop, ch 8, 5 dc in next loop, (ch 8, dc in next loop) 8 times, ch 8, repeat from * around, end with ch 4, trc in 3rd ch of beg ch.

Rnd 25: Ch 11, 5 dc in next loop, (ch 8, 5 dc in next loop) twice, * (ch 8, dc in next loop) 7 times, (ch 8, 5 dc in next loop) 3 times, repeat from * around, end with ch 4, trc in 3rd ch of beg ch.

Rnd 26: Ch 11, dc in next loop, * (ch 8, 5 dc in next loop) twice, (ch 8, dc in next loop) 8 times, repeat from * around, end with ch 4, trc in 3rd ch of beg ch.

Rnd 27: Ch 11, dc in next loop, (ch 8, dc in next loop) 3 times, * ch 8, dc in center of 5-dc section, ch 8, 5 dc in next loop, ch 8, dc in center of 5-dc section, (ch 8, dc in next loop) 9 times, repeat from * around, end with ch 4, trc in 3rd ch of beg ch.

Rnd 28: Ch 3, 4 dc in loop just made, * (ch 8, dc in next loop) 11 times, ch 8, 5 dc in next loop, repeat from * around, end with ch 4, trc in top of beg ch.

Rnd 29: Ch 3, 4 dc in loop just made, ch 8, 5 dc in next loop, * (ch 8, dc in next loop) 10 times, (ch 8, 5 dc in next loop) twice, repeat from * around, end with ch 4, trc in top of beg ch.

Rnd 30: Ch 3, 4 dc in loop just made, (ch 8, 5 dc in next loop) twice, * ch 8, dc in next loop 9 times, (ch 8, 5 dc in next loop) 3 times, repeat from * around, end with ch 4, trc in top of beg ch.

Rnd 31: Ch 11, * (5 dc in next loop, ch 8) twice, (ch 8, dc in next loop) 8 times, repeat from * around, end with ch 4, trc in 3rd ch of beg ch.

Rnd 32: Ch 11, dc in next loop, ch 8, dc in next loop, * ch 8, dc in center of next 5-dc section, ch 8, 5 dc in next loop, ch 8, dc in center of next 5-dc section, (ch 8, dc in next loop) 11 times, repeat from * around, end with ch 4, trc in 3rd ch of beg ch.

Rnd 33: Ch 11, dc in next loop, * ch 8, dc in next loop, repeat from * around, end with ch 8, sl st in 3rd ch of beg ch.

Rnd 34: Ch 1, * (8 sc in next loop) 4 times, turn, ch 8, sc in center of 8-sc loop just worked, (ch 8, sc in center of next 8-sc loop) twice, turn, 2 sc in loop just made, picot as follows: ch 3, sl st in first ch, 2 sc in same loop, ch 4, sc in center loop, ch 4, trc in next loop, turn, ch 8, sc in center of next loop, turn, picot, 4 sc, picot, 4 sc, picot in next loop, 4 sc in side of next loop, 2 sc, picot, 2 sc in side of next loop, repeat from * around, end with sc in beg ch 1. Sew a bead on each 5-dc section of the outer two rounds of clusters. (9 beads per cluster - 12 clusters).

Miniature ✥ Medallion Doily

MATERIALS:
Cordonnet Special #30 White -
    2 balls (216 yds per ball)
Size 12 steel hook

GAUGE:
5 rows dc = 1″
24 dc = 1″
Ch 6, sl st to make a
circle.

Rnd 1: Ch 3, 19 dc in ring (20).
Sl st in 3rd ch at beg.

Rnd 2: Ch 4, (dc, ch 1) in each
dc around. Join with sl st in
3rd ch at beg, sl st in first ch-1
sp.

Rnd 3: Ch 3, 2 dc in same sp,
(3 dc in next ch-1 sp) 3 times (4
groups) * ch 7, sk 1 sp, (3 dc
in next ch-1 sp) 4 times.
Repeat from *, end with ch 7,
sl st in top of beg ch. Fasten
off. Second medallion is
attached to the first as
follows: work 1 side of rnd 3,
ch 3, holding first medallion
behind second medallion,
wrong sides together, sc
through ch-7 corner of first
medallion, Ch 3, sk 1 sp, * 3
dc in next ch-1 sp of second
medallion, sc through first
medallion between next two
3-dc groups. Repeat from *
twice (attached 3 places), 3 dc

in next ch-1 sp (4th group), ch
3, attach corner with sc
through ch 7 of first medallion,
ch 3, continue around second
medallion completing rnd 3.
Fasten off. Fasten 5 medallions together in same way
making a row. Now start second row, one medallion at a
time, attatching to first row
and the next medallion of row
2. Corners of each medallion
are joined together: ch 3, sc
through center of ch-7 loops.
Work in same way until 10
rows of 5 medallions are set
together. Add remaining 6
medallions as in diagram. (56
medallions). Picot edge is
worked around outer edge of
entire piece as follows: attach
in any corner ch-7 sp, ch 1, sc
in same place, * ch 3, dc in
first dc, ch 3, sc in top of dc
just made (picot made), ch 3,
sk 2 dc, sc in sp between next
2 dc, ch 3, sk 3 dc, dc, picot
between next 2 dc, ch 3, sk
next 3 dc, sc between next 2
dc, ch 3, sk 2 dc, dc in last dc
of this medallion, picot, ch 3,
sc in joining of the 2 medallions. Repeat from * around
entire perimeter, end with ch 3,
sl st in beg sc. Fasten off.

# anciful Pinwheel Afghan

In this pattern we discover the truly decorative nature of the Victorian era. The fancy crocheted cover is the kind of treasure which brings us the lilt of another time.

MATERIALS:
Wondersheen Ivory - 43 balls (400 yards per ball)
Size 7 steel hook

Large Motif: Make 156 (each large motif is approximately 6 ½" in diameter). Ch 6, sl st in first ch to form a circle.

Rnd 1: Ch 3, 19 dc in circle, end with sl st in top of beg ch.

Rnd 2: Ch 3, (dc between next 2 dc) twice, * ch 6, sk 3 dcs, (dc between next 2 dc) 3 times, repeat from * twice, end with ch 6.

Note: Motif is worked in spiral - do not join each rnd. Mark beg of next rnd with a safety pin and move it for each rnd.

Rnd 3: * (Sc between next 2 dc of previous rnd) twice, 3 sc in ch-6 loop, ch 6, repeat from * around to pin (4 times), (5 sc in each section).

Rnd 4: * (Sk 1 sc, sc in next sc) 4 times, 3 sc in next loop, ch 6, repeat from * around (4 times), (7 sc each section).

Rnd 5: * (Sk 1 sc, sc in next sc) 6 times, 3 sc in next loop, ch 6, repeat from * around (4 times), (9 sc each section).

Rnds 6-11: Continue in same manner increasing 2 sc in each section until there are 21 sc.

Rnd 12: (Sk 1 sc, sc in next 19 sc, ch 6, sc in next loop, ch 6) 4 times.

Rnd 13: * Sk 1 sc, sc in next 17 sc, (ch 6, sc in next loop) twice, repeat from * 3 times.

Rnds 14-19: Continue in same manner decreasing 2 sc in each section and increasing 1 ch-6 loop in each rnd until there are 5 sc in each section and 9 ch-6 loops in each section.

Note: End final rnd - sk 1 sc, sc in next 3 scs. Fasten off. Set 2 large motifs together by joining the center 3 loops of one large motif to the center 3 loops of another large motif together along one side. You may wish to do this by whip stitching them together after completion of all motifs, or they may be joined on the last rnd (rnd 19) of large motif directions as follows: make 3 loops after sc section, (ch 3, sl st into corresponding loop of another large motif, ch 3, sc in next loop of first motif) 3 times. Join 4 motifs together, then fill the center by working a small motif.

Small motif: make 132 (each small motif is 3" in diameter). Ch 8, sl st in first ch to form a circle.

Rnd 1: Ch 6, (dc in center of circle, ch 3) 7 times, sl st in 3rd ch of beg.

Rnd 2: Ch 8, sk 1 loop from joining of any large motif, sc in next loop of large motif, turn, working in the ch-8 just made, sc in next 2 sts, hdc in next 2 sts, dc in next 2 sts, trc in next 2 sts, sc in next dc of small motif, (one spoke completed). Sk 1 loop, the sc section and 1 more loop, work next spoke in next loop of the same motif. Make 8 spokes, attaching 2 spokes on inner side of each of the 4 motifs.

Attach fringe to sides and bottom only. Each fringe consists of 4 strands each, 12" long folded together and tied in each ch loop around 3 sides of bed spread.

Sampler Doilies

As tiny as a coin, the smallest crocheted doily looks almost like a scrap of lace. Even the largest of these doilies is still only two inches square.

Now, you can display this beautiful crocheted sampler in your home.

MATERIALS: for square doily
DMC #100 Ivory or Ecru - 1 ball (472 yards per ball)
OR
Tatting thread #70 Ecru may be used - 1 ball (106 yards per ball)
Size 14 steel hook

Make a 6 petal rose (3 layers of petals) as follows: ch 6, sl st in first ch to form a circle.

Rnd 1: Ch 6, (dc in circle, ch 3) 5 times. Join with a sl st in the 3rd ch of beg ch 6 (6 sps).

Rnd 2: In each sp around, make 1 sc, 7 dc, 1 sc (6 petals).

Rnd 3: * Ch 5, sc in back of work in next dc of first rnd. Repeat from * around, end with ch 5, sc in same place as sl st on first rnd.

Rnd 4: In each loop around, make 1 sc, 8 dc, 1 sc. (6 petals).

Rnd 5: * Ch 6, working behind Rnd 4 petals, sc in sc between next 2 petals on 3rd rnd. Repeat from * around, end with sc between last and first petals.

Rnd 6: In each loop around, make 1 sc, 9 dc, 1 sc. (6 petals).

Rnd 7: * Ch 6, sl st in 4th ch from hook (picot made), ch 6, sl st in 4th ch from hook (picot made), ch 2, sk 4 dc, sc in next dc, (picot twice), ch 2, sc between next 2 sc (between petals). Repeat from * around, end with sc in beg ch of this

rnd. Note: from this point you will work in a spiral, do not join after each rnd.

Rnd 8: [* (Ch 6, sl st in 4th ch from hook) twice, ch 2, sc in center of next loop. Note: from now on this loop will be referred to as a picot loop. Repeat from * once, trc in next loop, ch 3, 10 trc over the trc just made, ch 3, sc in same loop where first trc was made], repeat 3 times.

Rnd 9: * (Make a picot loop, sc in center of next loop) twice, make a picot loop, sk 1 dc, sc in next dc, make a picot loop, (sk 3 dc, sc in next dc) twice, repeat from * around.

Rnd 10: * (Make a picot loop, sc in next loop) 4 times, trc in next loop, ch 3, 10 trc over the trc just made, ch 3, sc in same loop where first trc was made, repeat from * around.

Rnd 11: Repeat rnd 9 except have one more loop between the dc sections.

Rnd 12: Repeat rnd 10 except have one more loop between the dc sections in corners.

Rnd 13: * Ch 4, sc in next loop, ch 4, sl st in first ch (picot made), sc in same loop, repeat from * 5 times, ch 4, sc in first dc of group, make a picot, sc in same dc, make small picot loop as follows: (ch 4, sl st in first ch) twice, sc in center dc of group, make another small picot loop, sc in last dc of group. Repeat from beg of rnd working completely around, end with sl st in the beg ch. Fasten off.

MATERIALS: for six-sided doily
Tatting thread #70 Ivory - 1 ball
  (106 yards per ball)
Size 14 steel hook

Rnd 1: Ch 3, 5 dc in first ch made, end with sl st in 3rd ch of beg ch.

Rnd 2: Ch 2, 2 dc in same place, (ch 1, 3 dc in next dc) 5 times, end with ch 1, sl st in top of beg ch.

Rnd 3: Ch 2, dc in same place, dc in next dc, 2 dc in next dc, (ch 1, sk ch 1, 2 dc in next dc, 1 dc in next dc, 2 dc in next dc) around end with ch 1, sl st in top of beg ch.

Rnd 4: Ch 2, 2 dc in same place, dc in next 3 dcs, 2 dc in next st, (ch 1, sk ch-1, 2 dc in next dc, dc in next 3 dcs, 2 dc in next dc) around, end with ch 1, sl st in top of beg ch.

Rnd 5: Ch 2, dc in next 4 dcs, holding back last loop of next 2 dcs, dc over next 2 dcs (dec). Thread over and pull through all 3 loops, (ch 3, sc in ch-1 sp, ch 3, dec over next 2 dcs, dc in next 3 dcs, dec over next 2 dcs) around, end with ch 3, sc in ch-1 sp, ch 3, sl st in top of beg ch.

Rnd 6: Ch 2, dc in next 2 dcs, dec over next 2 dcs, * (ch 3, sc in next dc) twice, ch 3, dec over next 2 dcs, dc over next dc, dec over next 2 dcs, repeat from * around, end with ch 3, sl st in beg ch.

Rnd 7: Ch 2, dc over next 2 dcs, * (ch 3, sc in next sp) 3 times, ch 3, work dec over next 3 dcs, repeat from * around, end with ch 3, sl st in top of beg ch. Fasten off.

MATERIALS: for round doily
Tatting thread #70 Ecru - 1 ball
Size 14 steel hook
Ch 6, sl st to form a circle.

Rnd 1: Ch 2, 11 dc in circle, end with sl st in top of beg ch.

Rnd 2: Ch 2, dc in same place, 2 dc in each dc around, sl st in top of beg ch (24 sts).

Rnd 3: Ch 3, dc in next dc (ch 1, dc in next dc) around, end with ch 1, sl st in top of beg ch.

Rnd 4: Ch 2, dc in each dc around (48 sts).

Rnd 5: Ch 3, (sc in next dc, ch 2) around, end with sl st in first ch of beg.

Personalizing:

Look through your sewing box for trims and lace to make your crocheted doily sampler (photo page 46). We've added a pocket from an heirloom baby dress and two tiny satin rosebuds. Any treasures - buttons, jewelry, beads - added to our doilies will make your personal sampler unique.

owel dging

Linen - crisp and natural - is a traditional combination with the fine cottons used in crocheted edgings. Three distinctly different patterns are added to these towels to dress them up for special guests.

Buttons and Lace

MATERIALS:
Cordonnet Special #30 White -
  1 ball (216 yards per ball)
Size 12 steel hook

GAUGE:
5 rows dc = 1"
24 dc = 1"
Ch 17.

Row 1: Dc in 5th ch from hook, (ch 3, sk 3 sts, small shell of: dc, ch 1, dc, in next st) 3 times. Ch 3, turn.

Row 2: 3 dc in ch-1 sp of small shell, * ch 3, large shell (4 dc) in next ch-1 sp. Repeat from * once more. Ch 3, dc over next dc, ch 1, dc in 3rd ch of turning ch. Ch 4, turn.

Row 3: Sk ch-1 sp, dc over dc, ch 3, work small shell in first dc of large shell, (ch 3, small shell in next ch-3 sp) twice, ch 3, small shell in 3rd ch of turning ch, ch 3, turn.

Row 4: 3 dc in ch-1 sp, (ch 3, large shell in next ch-1 sp) 3 times, ch 3, dc over dc, ch 1, dc in 3rd st of turning ch, ch 4, turn.

Row 5: Sk ch-1 sp, dc over dc, ch 3, small shell in first dc of large shell (ch 3, small shell in next ch-3 sp) twice. Ch 3, turn. (Short row - do not work in remaining stitches). Repeat rows 2 through 5 for pattern until desired length.

Hairpin Lace

MATERIALS:
DMC Brilliant #842 Taupe - 1 ball (280 yards per ball)
Size 4 steel hook
2 ½" hairpin fork

GAUGE:

8 sc = 1"
4 rows sc = 1"

Work under both threads of each loop. (Double) wider center for hairpin lace sections or for more lacy center work under single thread. Make 1 strip of hairpin lace having 123 loops on each side of hairpin fork. Set aside.

Assembly: Ch 197, turn, holding hairpin lace in back of ch, sk 2 loops of hairpin, sc through next 2 loops, being careful always to have loops lying same direction, ch 3, sc in 6th ch, * ch 3, sc through 2 sk loops of hairpin, sk 2 loops, sc through next 2 loops, ch 3, sk 5 ch, sc in next ch. Repeat from * along entire ch, end with sc in 2 sk loops, sc through last 2 loops, sc in last ch, turn.

Base row for edge:

Row 1: Sl st in next 3 ch, (end of work), ch 1, sc in each ch across, end with sc only in last ch group.

Row 2: Ch 1, sc in next 7 scs, * ch 7, sk 5 scs, sc in next 3 scs, turn, 15 dc in ch loop just made, sk 2 scs, sl st in next 3 sts, turn, [ch 3, sc in first ch (picot made), sk 1dc, dc in next dc] 7 times, end with ch 3, sc in first ch (picot), sk 1 st, dc on side of sc worked in base row. Sk 2 sc on base row, sc in next 8 scs. Repeat from * to end of base row (10 scallops).

Finishing other side of hairpin lace: Ch 198, turn, sc in second ch and in each st across, turn. Holding hairpin lace section in back of sc section, ch 3. Repeat assembly row. Fasten off. Right sides facing, attach thread at top of edge just completed, ch 2, sk 2 sts, sc in next st, * ch 1, sk 2 sts, sc in next st. Repeat from * across. Fasten off.

Ribbons and Lace

MATERIALS:
Cordonnet #50 Natural - 1 ball
   (286 yards per ball)
Size 10 steel hook

GAUGE:
4 rows dc = 2½″
50 dc = 2½″

Heading: In this row, all picots are made by sc in 5th ch from hook. Ch 7, picot, ch 9, picot, ch 2, sl st in starting ch forming a loop, (ch 13, picot, ch 9, picot, ch 2, going back past last 2 picots, sl st in the 2nd ch from picot to make another loop) repeat for desired length, making the number of picot loops a multiple of 7 + 1. Fasten off.

Row 2: Turn, join to last picot loop between picots, (ch 7, sc in next picot loop) repeat to end. Ch 1, turn.

Row 3: (8 sc over next ch-7 sp) 4 times, * ch 10, turn, sl st in 8th sc from hook, ch 1, turn, 13 sc over 10-ch loop, (8 sc over next space) 7 times. Repeat from * to end. Fasten off.

Shells: Join to 1st sc on one 13-sc loop, (ch 4, sc in next 2 sc) 3 times, ch 4, sc in last sc, (ch 4, sc in next 2 sc) 3 times, sl st to center of next sp, ch 5, turn, sc in last 4-ch loop, (ch 5, sc in next loop) 6 times, ch 5,

sk 4 sc on heading, sl st in next 4 sc. Ch 3, turn, sc in last loop, (ch 6, sc in next loop) 7 times, ch 3, sl st in next 4th sc on heading. Ch 7, turn, sc in last 6-ch loop, (ch 7, sc in next loop) 6 times, ch 7, sl st on heading at end of last row, sl st to center of next sp on heading. Ch 5, sc in 4th ch from hook for a picot, ch 3, turn, sc in last loop, * (ch 6, sc in 4th ch from hook) twice, ch 3, sc in next loop. Repeat from * 6 times. Ch 6, picot, ch 2, sl st in center of next sp on heading. Turn, (ch 6, picot, ch 7, picot, ch 3, sc in center of next picot loop) 6 times, joining final picot loop to heading at end of last row. Fasten off. Make this same shell around each added loop on heading.

EDGE: Join thread to center of 1st space on heading, * ch 5, sc in 1st picot loop, (ch 11, sc in next picot loop) 7 times, ch 5, sc in center of next sp on heading, sc in each sc to center of next sp. Repeat from * to end. Fasten off.

Row 2: Join to 1st sc on heading at opposite end, (4 dc, 1 hdc, and 1 sc) over next ch-5 loop, (1 sc, 1 hdc, 5 dc, ch 5, sl st in last dc for a picot, 5 dc, 1 hdc and 1 sc) over each of
(continued)

next 5 loops, [(1 sc, 1 hdc, 10 dc, 1 hdc and 1 sc) over next loop] twice, (1 sc, 1 hdc and 4 dc) over next ch-5 loop, sl st in center sc on heading between loops, (4 dc, 1 hdc, and 1 sc) over next ch-5 loop, (1 sc, 1 hdc and 5 dc) over half of next loop, ch 3, turn, sl st in center of corresponding scallop on last shell, ch 1, turn, 5 sc over ch-3, sl st in last dc, (5 dc, 1 hdc and 1 sc) over balance of loop, (1 sc, 1 hdc and 5 dc) over half of next loop, ch 4, turn, 1 tr trc in 2nd of 5 sc on connecting bar, (ch 4, tr trc in next sc) twice, ch 4, sl st in center of next scallop, ch 1, turn, 6 sc over each 4-ch, sl st in last dc. Ch 5, turn, sk last 10 sc , 3 dtrc in a single loop of next sc holding last loop of each dtrc on hook thread over and pull through all 4 loops on hook at once (a cluster), (ch 5, a 3 dtrc cluster in next sc) 3 times, ch 5, sl st in center of same scallop on shell. Ch 1, turn, (1 sc, 1 hdc, 4 dc, 1 hdc and 1 sc) over each ch-5 sp, sl st in last dc on scallop, (5 dc, 1 hdc and 1 sc) over balance of same scallop, (1 sc, 1 hdc, 5 dc, a picot, 5 dc, 1 hdc and 1 sc) over each of next 3 loops. Repeat from * to end. Finish last shell with a picot in each scallop the same as 1st shell.

TINY BALLS: (Make 3)
Size 14 steel hook
Tatting thread #70 ecru

Note: Use blunt end of crochet hook to stuff cotton into ball Ch 4, sl st in first ch to form a circle. Ch 1, work 8 sc in circle, continue working around in spiral, work 2 sc in each sc (16 scs), work 5 rnds maintaining 16 scs. Next rnd: (sc in next 2 scs, sk 1 sc) around. Stuff with 1/2 cotton ball. Next rnd: sc in every other sc, sl st in last sc to pull tog for closure. Ch 20. Join with sl st as desired on edging.

Materials:

One 18″ × 27″ piece of linen (ivory and mauve); matching thread
One 3½″ × 18″ piece of pink linen
Five small buttons
Assorted 18″ lengths of ribbon and flat lace

Directions:

1. On left hand towel (see photo, page 46), place band of pink linen 3″ above lower edge of towel. Fold edges under ¼″. Slipstitch to towel.

2. Turn under ¼″ hem on all edges of linen. Slipstitch hem.

3. Attach lace, trim and buttons as desired (see photo for placement).

Filet Crochet House

As seasons come and go, the Filet Crochet House reminds us that home and family remain constant. Our crochet is framed over burgundy fabric, but you will want to choose a color to accent your home.

SIZE: 20 ½″ × 22 ½″

MATERIALS:
Cebelia #30 Ecru - 2 balls (563 yards per ball)
Size 7 steel hook

KEY:

□ 1 Block = 3 dc
◨ 1 Space = ch 2, dc

Note: There are always dc over dc and 2 dc in each ch 2 open space.

Ch 243.

Row 1: Dc in 9th ch from hook, (ch 2, sk 2 ch, dc in next ch) across (79 spaces).

Rows 2-7: Ch 5, turn, dc in 1st dc of previous row, ch 2 dc in next dc, repeat across row. To end row, ch 2, sk 2 dc in turning ch. Dc in next ch dc.

Row 8: Continue following graph.

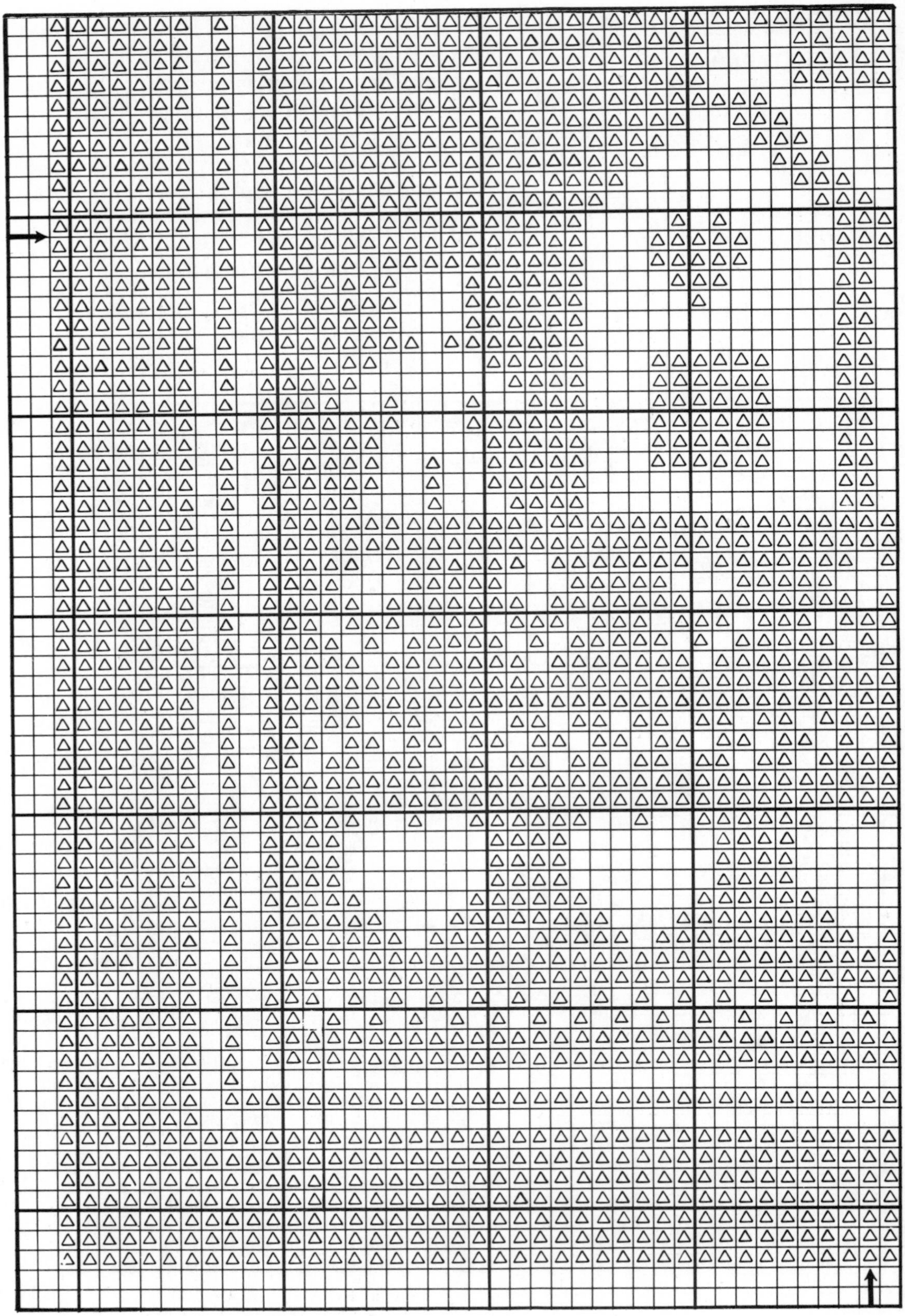

Elegant Opera Bag

With just a little loosening of one's imagination, it becomes easy to "see" the lady who might have carried this handsome bag. And now you can have your very own to carry or display along with this beautiful dresser set and two jar lid trims.

MATERIALS:
Cebelia #30 Ecru Natural - 3 balls (563 yards per ball)
Size 10 steel hook
8 cotton balls
Safety pin

GAUGE:
12 dc = 1"
4 rows dc = 1"

TINY BALLS: (Make 2) Ch 3, sl st to form a circle. Ch 1, work 8 sc in circle, continue working around in a spiral, work 2 sc in each sc (16 scs). Work 3 rnds maintaining 16 scs, next rnd (sc in next 2 scs, sk 1 sc) around. Stuff with ½ cotton ball. Next rnd - sc in every other sc, sl st in last sc to pull together for closure. Fasten off. Leave 4" of thread for sewing in place later. Note: use blunt end of crochet hook to push cotton into ball.

BALLS: (Make 5) Ch 3, sl st in first ch to form a circle, ch 1, work 8 sc in circle, next rnd work 2 sc in each sc around (16 scs). Next round work (2 sc in next sc, 1 sc in next sc) around (24 scs). Maintain 24 sts working around 5 rnds. Next rnd (sc in next 2 scs, sk 1 sc) (16 scs). Stuff with cotton ball. Sc in every other sc around, close with sl st. Fasten off. Leave 4" of thread.

BAG: (Make 2)

Rnd 1: Ch 4, sl st to form a circle, ch 1, work 10 sc in circle. Continue working in a spiral.

Rnd 2: Work 2 sc in each sc around (mark end of rnd with a saftey pin) (20 scs).

Rnd 3: (2 sc in next sc, sc in next sc) around (30 scs).

Rnd 4: Sc in next sc, (2 sc in next sc, sc in next 2 scs) around (40 sts).

Rnd 5: Sc in each sc around (40 sts).

Rnd 6: (Sc in next 4 scs, 2 sc in next sc) around (48 scs).

Rnd 7: Sc in each sc around (48 scs).

Rnd 8: (Sc in next 7 scs, 2 sc in next sc) around (54 scs).

Rnd 9: Sc in each sc around (54 scs).

Rnd 10: (Sc in next 8 scs, 2 sc in next sc) around (60 scs). Turn. Work 5 sections independently, like spokes, as follows:

First Section:

Row 1: Ch 1, sc in back loop only of next 12 scs, turn.

Row 2: Ch 1, sc in back loop only of next 13 scs, turn. Note: the increase occurs by working sc in the beg ch 1, as well as in each sc.

Row 3: Ch 1, sc in back loop only of next 14 scs, turn.

Rows 4-10: Work in same manner, increasing 1 sc each row. At the end of 10 rows there should be 21 scs. Work sc in each row down side of section just worked (10 sc). Work other 4 sections in same manner, except do not work down side of last section.

Rnd 1: Working in rnd, * (ch 6, sl st in 4th ch from hook to form a picot) twice, ch 3, sc in 1st sc of next section, (ch 5, sk 2 scs, sc in next sc) 7 times, repeat from * around, end with sl st in beg ch.

Note: The (ch 6, picot) twice, ch 3, will hereafter be referred to as double picot loop or dpl in the instructions.

Rnd 2: [Dpl, ch 3, sc between picots in next loop, * dpl, ch 3, sc in next loop, sk 1 loop, repeat from * 3 times], repeat around, mark last loop worked with a safety pin.

Rnd 3: Dpl, ch 3, sc in center of next loop, * ch 8, sc in center of next loop, (dpl, ch 3, sc in center of next loop) 4 times, repeat from * around, end with work 1 loop beyond pin loop. Move pin into this loop.

Rnd 4: [Dpl, ch 3, 12 dc in the ch-8 loop, * dpl, ch 3, sc in center of next loop, repeat from * 3 times,] repeat around,

end with dpl, ch 3, sc in loop beyond pin. Move pin to this loop just made.

Rnd 5: * Dpl, sc between 1st and 2nd dc of group, dpl, sk 5 dc, sc between next 2 dc (center of group), dpl, sk 5 dc, sc between last 2 dc of group, (dpl, sc in center of next loop) 5 times, repeat from * around, work dpl, sc in next loop beyond pin loop twice, move pin to this last loop.

Rnd 6: * Ch 10, sc in next loop, note the ch without picots should always be directly above the sp that lies between the 5 spoke-like sections. (Dpl, sc in next loop) 7 times, repeat from * around to pin.

Rnd 7: * Dpl, 12 dc in ch-10 loop, (dpl, sc in next loop) 7 times, repeat from * around to pin.

Rnd 8: * Dpl, sc between 1st and 2nd dc of group, dpl, sk 5 dc, sc in center of group, (dpl, sc in center of next loop) 8 times, repeat from * around, end at pin. Fasten off. Front of the bag is now completed. Repeat to make back.

Joining: Place the 2 sections together, right sides out. Attach thread in 2nd dpl loop above the 12 dc group. Work through both sections, sc in

same loop. Dpl, sc in next loop around 4 sections, stopping in the first loop above 12-dc sections. Leave 1 section open for top of bag. Do not fasten off.

Top Edge: Work through one section only.

Rnd 1: (Beading rnd) (Ch 6, sc in center of next loop) around top of bag opening, end with ch 3, trc in sc. Put a pin in last loop just made.

Rnd 2: (Beading rnd) Sc in same loop, (ch 6, sc in next loop) around, end with ch 3, trc in beg sc.

Rnds 3-4: (Dpl, sc in next loop) around. Fasten off.

Finishing: Sew 1 tiny ball to center of front and back of bag. Sew 1 ball to center of first 12 dc section on each side of front of bag. Sew 1 ball at outside edge of bag near center of 12 dc sections of center bottom of bag and each side.

Drawstring: Make ch 50″ long. Sc in 2nd ch and in each ch to end. Lace through top of bag between 2 beading rnds. Join drawstring together, fasten off leaving 6″ thread to attach 1 ball. Fold drawstring in half, attach another ball to other side of drawstring. Tie a knot about 2½″ in from each ball.

Fancy Lid Cover

SIZE: Fits regular size jar lid

MATERIALS:
Cordonnet #50 Natural - 1 ball
  (286 yards per ball)
Size 12 steel hook

GAUGE:

7 rows dc = 1"
15 dc = 1"

Ch 55.

Row 1: Dc in 7th ch from hook, (sk 2 chs, dc in next ch) 16 times (17 sp). Turn.

Row 2: Ch 5, dc over dc, (ch 2, dc over dc) 16 times. Repeat this row 15 more times.

Rnd 1: Work around entire square: ch 1, 3 sc in first space, (2 sc in each sp to corner, work 5 sc in corner) repeat around, end with 2 sc in last corner, sl st in beg ch.

Rnd 2: Ch 3, dc in corner sp, ch 12, 2 dc in same sp, * (ch 1, sk 1 sc, dc in next sc) 16 times, (2 dc, ch 12, 2 dc) in corner st, repeat from * around, omit last (2 dc, ch 12, 2 dc) on last repeat, end with sl st in top of beg ch.

Rnd 3: Sl st into ch-12 loop, ch 4, * 19 dtrc in corner sp, sk 2 sps, 3 dc in next sp, (sk 1 sp, ch 2, 3 dc in next sp) 6 times, sk 2 sp, repeat from * around, end with sl st in top of beg ch.

Rnd 4: Ch 5, (trc in next st, ch 1) 18 times, * sk 3 dc, (3 dc in ch-2 sp, ch 2) 6 times, omit ch 2 on last time, (trc, ch 1) 19 times around corner, repeat from * around, end with sl st in 4th ch of beg.

Rnd 5: Ch 6, (trc over next trc, ch 2) 17 times, trc over last trc, * sk 3 dcs, (3 dc, ch 2, in next ch-2 sp), 5 times, omit ch 2 on last time, (trc over trc, ch 1) 18 times, trc over last trc, repeat from * around, end with sl st in 4th ch of beg.

Rnd 6: Ch 7, (trc over next trc, ch 3) 17 times, trc over last trc, * sk 3 dcs, (3 dc, ch 2 in next sp,) 4 times, omit ch 2 on last time, (trc over trc, ch 3) 18 times, trc over last trc, repeat from * around, end with sl st in 4th ch of beg.

Rnd 7: Ch 8, (trc over next trc, ch 4) 17 times, trc over last trc, * sk 3 dcs, (3 dc, ch 2 in next sp) 3 times, omit ch 2 on last time, (trc over trc ch 4) 18 times, trc over last trc, repeat from * around, end with sl st in 4th ch of beg.

Rnd 8: Repeat rnd 7, except ch 5 between trcs, omitting one 3 dc section.

Rnd 9: Repeat rnd 7, except ch 6 between trcs, having only 1 section of 3 dc.

Rnd 10: Ch 10, sl st in 4th ch from hook (picot made), ch 2, [* trc over trc, picot, ch 2, repeat from * to 3 dc, 2 dc over first dc of group, 1 dc over center dc, 2 dc over last dc], repeat around, end with sl st in top of beg ch. Fasten off.

Ruffled Lid Cover

SIZE: Fits regular size jars.

MATERIALS:
Wondersheen Ivory - 1 skein
(400 yards per skein)
Size 4 steel hook

GAUGE: 10 dc = 1"
2 rows dc = 1"

LINKS: Ch 3, dc in first ch, * ch 3, dc between ch and dc. (2 links made). Repeat from * until desired number of links are made. Make 20 ch 3, dc, links, turn. Work on dc side.

Row 1: Sl st in first link, ch 4, dc in same link, * ch 1, shell of (dc, ch 1, dc) in next link. Repeat from * across.

Row 2: Ch 3, turn, 4 dc in first ch-1 sp, * sk 1 sp, 5 dc in next sp. Repeat from * across.

Row 3: Ch 6, turn, sc in 3rd ch from hook (picot made), dc in first dc of row below, * ch 1, shell in next dc, ch 1, dc, ch 3, sc in top of dc just made (picot made), dc in same st. Repeat from * across, fasten off. [dc, picot, dc in first dc of 5-dc group of row below, ch 1, shell in next dc, (dc, picot, dc) in next dc, ch 1, shell in next dc, ch 1, (dc, picot, dc) in next dc]. Repeat across. Fasten off.

Finishing: Run ribbon through row 1. Tie in a bow.

Vintage Dresser Scarf

SIZE: 14½" × 7"

Complete two **Fancy Lid Cover** motifs, eliminating rnd 10 on one motif.

Joining two motifs together: starting with rnd 10 on incomplete motif, ch 10, sl st in 4th ch from hook (picot made), ch 2,*trc over trc, ch 6, sl st in 4th ch from hook - picot, ch 2, repeat from * until 13 picot loops are made, * * trc over next trc, ch 4, sl st in center of the 6th picot up from 5-dc section of completed motif, repeat from * *, in next picot 4 times more, joining the next four loops, trc in trc just before 3-dc section, ch 6, sl st in 4th ch from hook, ch 2, 2 dc over first dc of group, 1 dc over center dc, 2 dc over last dc, ch 6, sl st in 4th ch from hook, ch 2. Repeat between * * in next 5 picot loops, then continue as for rnd 10 to completion of rnd.

Stitches

Hemstitching

The pieces in this book which call for hemstitching have been stitched on a machine. Some sewing machines have a hemstitching attachment. If you do not have access to one, inquire at your crochet supplier about a person who does professional hemstitching.

Base Chain

This is a series of chain stitches, which normally begins with a loop secured by a slip knot.

Slip Knot

1. Make a loop; hook another loop through it.

2. Tighten gently and slide the knot up to the hook.

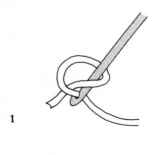

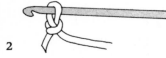

Chain Stitch (ch)

1. Beginning with a slip knot on your hook, wrap the yarn over the hook.

2. Pull the yarn through the loop. One ch is completed.

Repeat until desired chain length is reached.

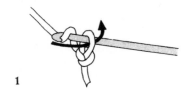

Note: To count chains correctly, do not count the initial slip loop as a chain.

Slip Stitch (sl st)

1. Beginning with hook in the initial slip loop of the base chain, insert the hook into the 2nd chain from the hook. Wrap the yarn over the hook and pull through the chain and the loop on the hook in one movement. One sl st is completed.

2. Continue in the same way to end.

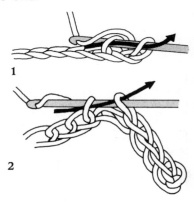

Single Crochet (sc)

1. Beginning with hook in the initial slip loop of the base chain, insert the hook into the 2nd chain from the hook. Wrap the yarn over the hook and pull through the chain (2 loops on hook).

2. Wrap the yarn again and pull the yarn through both loops on the hook. One sc is completed.

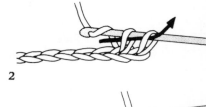

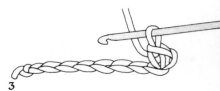

92

Half-Double Crochet (hdc)

1. Beginning with hook in the initial slip loop of the base chain, wrap the yarn over the hook and insert the hook into the 3rd chain from the hook.

2. Wrap the yarn over the hook and pull through chain (3 loops on hook). Wrap the yarn again.

3. Pull through all 3 loops on hook. One hdc is completed.

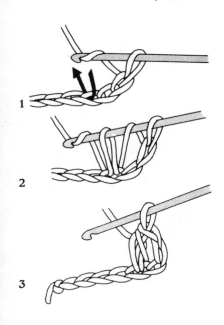

Double Crochet (dc)

1. Beginning with hook in the initial slip loop of the base chain, wrap the yarn over the hook and insert the hook into the
4th chain from the hook.

2. Wrap the yarn over the hook and pull through chain (3 loops on hook). Wrap the yarn again.

3. Pull through the first 2 loops only (2 loops on hook) and wrap the yarn again.

4. Pull through the last 2 loops on the hook.

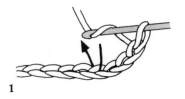

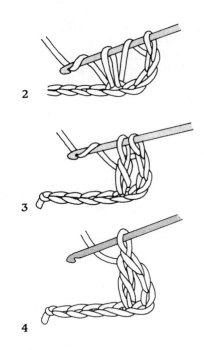

Treble Crochet (trc)

1. Beginning with hook in the initial slip loop of the base chain, wrap the yarn over the hook twice and insert the hook into the 5th chain from the hook.

2. Wrap the yarn over the hook and pull through chain (4 loops on hook). Wrap the yarn again.

3. Pull through the first 2 loops only (3 loops remain). Wrap the yarn again.

4. Pull through the next 2 loops only (2 loops remain). Wrap the yarn again.

5. Pull through the last 2 loops on hook. One trc is completed.

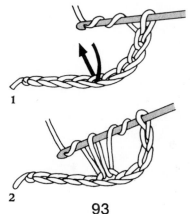

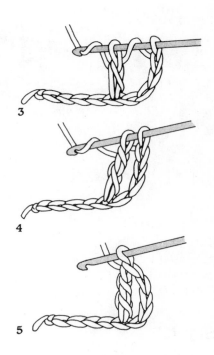

Longer Basic Stitches

Longer basic stitches - usually called Double Treble (d trc) and Triple Treble (t trc) - are made by wrapping the yarn 3 for d trc and 4 for t trc times over the hook at the beginning. To complete the stitch, wrap and pull through 2 loops each step.

Size

The size listed in the instructions is the finished size of our models shown on the photograph pages. Size is not included on projects where a difference would not matter. In most cases, size will be based on your personal needs, so keep your measurements in mind when working on a project.

Materials

In the instructions for each project, you will find a list of materials which were used to finish the pieces shown on the photographed pages. Other items you will need on hand are a tape measure, scissors, pins, and a blunt ended needle.

If you decide to follow our suggestions, your trip to the yarn shop should be simple. However, if you substitute another yarn or hook, be aware of the differences in the amount of yarn you will need and be sure to check your gauge.

Gauge

The most important single factor for successfully completing a pattern is obtaining the "gauge" or "tension" called for in the instructions. The gauge is specified as number of stitches and a number of rows. Stitch gauge is generally more important than row gauge.

Before starting any pattern, you should make a square sample swatch about 4″ wide using the yarn you have chosen, the correct stitch and the suggested hook size. When you have completed the sample, lay the square down on a flat surface and measure it horizontally for stitch gauge, and vertically for row gauge.

If you do not obtain the same gauge as indicated in the pattern, your work will not come to the measurement given. To attain the correct gauge, make another sample with a different hook size. A larger hook will give you fewer stitches and a smaller hook will give you more.

Abbreviations

beg	beginning
ch	chain
ch-	refers to chain previously made
cont	continue
dc	double crochet
dec	decrease
d trc	double treble crochet
inc	increase
rem	remaining
rep	repeat
rnd	round
sc	single crochet
sk	skip
sl st	slip stitch
st	stitch
trc	treble crochet
tr trc	triple treble crochet
yo	yarn over

Asterisks (*) - used to mark the beginning of a set of instructions that are to be repeated.

Brackets [ ] - instructions are put inside brackets and these are to be repeated the number of times stated.

Base Chain - the length of chain made at the beginning of a piece of chochet as a basis for constructing the fabric.

Decrease - lessening the number of stitches in a row.

Increase - adding to the number of stitches in a row

Picot - a run of chain stitches fixed into a decorative loop to form a simple edging.

Yarn Over - the instruction to wrap the yarn from the ball over the hook; always done in a counter-clockwise direction, unless otherwise stated.